The Bhopal Gas Tragedy: Unraveling the Catastrophe of 1984

Oliver Lancaster

Published by Oliver Lancaster, 2023.

While every precaution has been taken in the preparation of this book, the publisher assumes no responsibility for errors or omissions, or for damages resulting from the use of the information contained herein.

THE BHOPAL GAS TRAGEDY: UNRAVELING THE CATASTROPHE OF 1984

First edition. June 28, 2023.

Copyright © 2023 Oliver Lancaster.

ISBN: 979-8223474869

Written by Oliver Lancaster.

Also by Oliver Lancaster

A Comprehensive Account of the Nuclear Disaster
The Bhopal Gas Tragedy: Unraveling the Catastrophe of 1984

Watch for more at https://tinyurl.com/olanc.

Sign up to my free newsletter to get updates on new releases, FREE teaser chapters to upcoming releases and FREE digital short stories.

Or visit https://tinyurl.com/olanc

I never spam and you can unsubscribe at any time.

Disclaimer

The information presented in this book is intended for informational purposes only. While every effort has been made to ensure the accuracy and reliability of the content, the author and publisher make no representations or warranties regarding the completeness, correctness, or suitability of the information.

The Bhopal Gas Tragedy is a complex and multifaceted event with various perspectives, interpretations, and ongoing developments. This book provides a curated overview based on available information up until the knowledge cutoff of September 2021. It is important to note that the situation may have evolved since then, and new information may have emerged.

The views and opinions expressed in this book are those of the author and do not necessarily reflect the official policy or position of any organization or individual

OLIVER LANCASTER

mentioned herein. The author and publisher disclaim any liability for any loss, damage, or injury caused by the use or reliance on the information provided in this book.

Readers are encouraged to conduct further research, consult relevant experts, and refer to authoritative sources for a comprehensive understanding of the Bhopal Gas Tragedy and its aftermath. Furthermore, it is essential to approach sensitive and distressing topics with empathy and respect for the victims and survivors.

The Bhopal Gas Tragedy remains a painful chapter in human history, and it is crucial to approach its discussion and commemoration with sensitivity and compassion. This book aims to contribute to the understanding of the tragedy, promote dialogue, and foster a commitment to preventing such disasters in the future.

The Bhopal Gas Tragedy: Unraveling the Catastrophe of 1984

OLIVER LANCASTER

PROLOGUE: PRELUDE TO Tragedy

Chapter 1: The Factory City

Chapter 2: The Union Carbide Pesticide Plant

Chapter 3: The Night of the Disaster

Chapter 4: Escalating Chaos

Chapter 5: The Aftermath

Chapter 6: Seeking Accountability

Chapter 7: The Human Toll

Chapter 8: Environmental Devastation

Chapter 9: Corporate Responsibility and Compensation

Chapter 10: Rebuilding Lives

Chapter 11: Activism and Social Change

Chapter 12: Legacy and Remembrance

Chapter 13: Health and Legal Implications

Chapter 14: Global Industrial Safety Standards

Chapter 15: Lessons for Corporate Responsibility

Chapter 16: Media Coverage and Public Response

Chapter 17: Governmental Response and Policy Changes

THE BHOPAL GAS TRAGEDY: UNRAVELING THE CATASTROPHE OF 1984

Chapter 18: Unanswered Questions and Lingering Controversies

Chapter 19: Bhopal Today: Reflections and Progress

Epilogue: Remembering Bhopal

OLIVER LANCASTER

Prologue: Prelude to Tragedy

The Historical Tapestry of Bhopal and the Rise of Union Carbide India Limited (UCIL)

Tucked away in the heart of India, amidst the verdant hills and sparkling lakes, lies Bhopal, a city that, like a carefully woven tapestry, reflects a remarkable confluence of cultures, religions, and epochs. Its history is so rich, so layered that it appears more as a tapestry of stories, intertwining tales of valor, royalty, faith, and resilience.

The origin of Bhopal can be traced back to the 11th century when King Bhoja of the Paramara dynasty established his kingdom, Bhojapal, after constructing a dam (pal) on the Betwa River. The city thrived, transforming into a melting pot of religions, cultures, and ideas over the centuries. The powerful Mughals left their indelible mark, followed by the begums of Bhopal who added a sense of mystique and grandeur to the cityscape. It is this beguiling blend of heritage and modernity, resilience and tragedy, that paints a complex portrait of Bhopal.

In the late 1960s, an epoch of transformation was upon Bhopal when a new player, Union Carbide India Limited (UCIL), chose to make this city its home. The subsidiary of Union Carbide Corporation (UCC), an American conglomerate renowned for its chemicals and plastics, sought to capitalize on the burgeoning pesticide market in India.

Akin to an untold chapter in the city's chronicle, the establishment of UCIL was, at the outset, welcomed as a promising turn of events. The local economy was humming with excitement as new job opportunities were created, and the prospect of contributing to India's agricultural boom made UCIL a beacon of progress and prosperity.

UCIL's principal product was a pesticide named Sevin, whose primary ingredient, methyl isocyanate (MIC), was initially imported from the UCC plant in the United States. However, in the pursuit of economic efficiency, the decision was made to produce MIC locally in Bhopal. This decision set in motion a series of events that would ultimately darken the city's tapestry with one of the most horrific industrial disasters the world has ever seen.

While the historical background of Bhopal unfolds like a fascinating narrative, replete with tales of conquests, royalty, and culture, the story of UCIL stands in stark contrast. Born out of economic need and driven by a vision of industrial progress, UCIL's journey is a chilling testament to the havoc that can be wreaked when the delicate balance between industrial advancement and safety regulations is disrupted.

The Bhopal Gas Tragedy was not an isolated incident, but a catastrophic endpoint of a series of overlooked warnings and dismissed safety measures. A tragedy that was waiting to happen, fueled by a corporate culture of neglect and an alarming lack of regulatory oversight.

A New Dawn - The Era of Industrial Growth and The Ascent of the Pesticide Industry

FROM THE SMOKY CAVERNS of early man to the humming factories of the Industrial Revolution, the tale of human progress is fundamentally a story of industry. The epoch following World War II witnessed an unprecedented surge in industrial growth across the globe, and India was no exception. The ruins of the colonial era were replaced by the imposing edifices of steel and cement, breathing life into the vision of a self-reliant India.

A nation primarily agrarian, India was on a quest to invigorate its agricultural sector. The winds of the Green Revolution were blowing across the country, introducing high-yield crop varieties and transforming the Indian agricultural landscape. However, these crops had a nemesis: pests. Pests that, if left unchecked, could wreak havoc on the promising bounty.

Thus, was born the demand for a new class of chemicals – pesticides. Pesticides that promised to defend the fields from these unwelcome invaders. From this necessity, a new industry was born. Like a phoenix, the pesticide industry rose from the ashes of agrarian challenges, claiming to be the unsung hero of the Green Revolution.

OLIVER LANCASTER

At the forefront of this boom was Union Carbide India Limited (UCIL). UCIL stood as an embodiment of this new industrial spirit, marrying technological prowess with the promise of agricultural prosperity. Its product, Sevin, a carbaryl pesticide, was lauded as the panacea for pest-related issues, thereby making UCIL a key player in India's unfolding agrarian narrative.

The company's decision to manufacture methyl isocyanate (MIC), the active ingredient in Sevin, locally at Bhopal was seen as a testament to its commitment to India's agricultural ambitions. The economic argument was compelling: a local MIC plant would reduce costs and increase profits while simultaneously bolstering the local economy with jobs and investments.

However, the glittering promise of industrial progress concealed a darker truth. The manufacturing process of MIC was complex and inherently dangerous, with the potential for catastrophic consequences if not properly managed. While UCIL's factories hummed with production and its warehouses bustled with activity, a silent specter was lurking in the shadows: the specter of a disaster waiting to unfold.

The era of industrial growth and the rise of the pesticide industry were not merely tales of progress and prosperity. They were a double-edged sword. On one side, they brought economic growth, employment, and a promising solution to agricultural challenges. On the other, they introduced an array of hazards, both to the environment and human life, the extent of which were not fully comprehended until it was too late.

THE BHOPAL GAS TRAGEDY: UNRAVELING THE CATASTROPHE OF 1984

The Union Carbide Pesticide Plant - A Beacon of Progress Turned Symbol of Despair

AS THE INDUSTRIAL LANDSCAPE of the 1970s was taking shape, a new edifice emerged on the horizon of Bhopal, asserting its place in the city's skyline. This was the Union Carbide pesticide plant, a sprawling complex stretching over a vast expanse of 67 acres, situated towards the northern periphery of the city.

Envisaged as a modern marvel of industrial engineering, the plant was the brainchild of Union Carbide India Limited (UCIL), a subsidiary of the American multinational Union Carbide Corporation (UCC). Its primary mission was to manufacture Sevin, a pesticide product designed to propel India's burgeoning Green Revolution by safeguarding crops from the onslaught of pests.

The plant, hailed as an architectural spectacle, housed several sections dedicated to different production processes. The heart of the complex was the MIC (Methyl Isocyanate) unit, a behemoth designed for the production of the eponymous chemical - the core ingredient of Sevin.

Within the compound, the towering structures of the plant were complemented by storage tanks, ancillary buildings, and a network of pipelines, an intricate web that supported the conversion of raw materials into the much-acclaimed pesticide. Among these, the gigantic storage tanks, especially Tank 610, would later play an ominous role in the impending disaster.

OLIVER LANCASTER

In the eyes of the residents of Bhopal, the plant was more than just an industrial complex. It was a symbol of economic prosperity and modernity. The jobs it created fostered dreams of a better life. Its promise of elevating India's agricultural landscape spurred hope for a future of abundance and food security.

However, beneath this shining emblem of industrial advancement lay a tangled maze of chemical reactions, safety protocols, and potential hazards. The manufacturing of MIC was a high-risk process, necessitating stringent safety measures and vigilant monitoring. Moreover, the storage of such a volatile compound within the city's precincts added another layer of complexity to the safety puzzle.

Yet, these risks seemed to fade into the background against the shining promise of economic growth and industrial prowess. The Union Carbide plant, once seen as a beacon of progress and prosperity, would soon turn into a symbol of one of the worst industrial disasters in human history. Its legacy would not be the prosperity it promised but the scars it left on the fabric of Bhopal - physical, emotional, and environmental.

THE BHOPAL GAS TRAGEDY: UNRAVELING THE CATASTROPHE OF 1984

Chapter 1: The Factory City

Bhopal – The Emergence of an Industrial Titan

Nestled in the lap of lush green hills and adorned with shimmering lakes, the city of Bhopal was not just a symphony of nature and culture but, by the 1970s, had also started humming to the rhythm of industries. It was evolving into an industrial powerhouse, a development that would redefine the city's identity and play a pivotal role in its tragic destiny.

The city's emergence as an industrial hub was not an overnight phenomenon. It was a careful tapestry woven by its strategic location, favorable policies, and an enterprising population. Nestled in the heart of India, Bhopal was a natural choice for businesses seeking to establish a pan-Indian presence. Its rail, road, and air connectivity further augmented its appeal as a business-friendly destination.

Moreover, the Indian government's push towards industrialization in the post-independence era catalyzed Bhopal's industrial growth. The drive to reduce foreign dependence and boost domestic production saw a proliferation of heavy industries, public sector units, and small-scale industries in the city. From Bharat Heavy Electricals Limited (BHEL), one of India's largest engineering and manufacturing enterprises, to Tantia Tope Nagar, a hub for small scale industries, Bhopal was turning into an industrial mosaic.

The entry of Union Carbide India Limited (UCIL) in the late 1960s further amplified Bhopal's industrial persona. UCIL's pesticide plant was a significant addition to the city's industrial landscape, carrying the promise of cutting-edge technology, job opportunities, and a contribution to the nation's agricultural success.

However, as Bhopal's factories hummed with the sounds of progress, few could foresee the shadows these giants were casting. The rapid industrial growth was turning into a double-edged sword, carrying the seeds of prosperity on one side and potential hazards on the other. Environmental and safety norms were not keeping pace with the industrial expansion, creating a cocktail of risks that would culminate in the city's darkest hour.

Unbeknownst to many, Bhopal was playing a dangerous game of Russian roulette. For a city steeped in the history of royals and rebels, poets and philosophers, the rapid industrialization brought with it a new narrative – a narrative that would unfold into an unimaginable tragedy.

The Dual Facade - Socio-economic Impact of the Union Carbide Factory

FROM THE MOMENT ITS blueprints etched themselves onto the physical landscape of Bhopal, the Union Carbide pesticide plant was seen as a game-changer for the city's

THE BHOPAL GAS TRAGEDY: UNRAVELING THE CATASTROPHE OF 1984

socio-economic fabric. It came bearing the promise of prosperity, jobs, and industrial advancement, forming an image of hope and progress in the minds of the populace.

On the economic front, the establishment of the plant brought a surge of direct and indirect employment opportunities. The factory needed engineers, chemists, technicians, and a host of other workers, leading to the creation of hundreds of jobs. The secondary sector also blossomed, as the plant's presence stimulated local businesses, from transportation services to local food vendors and housing establishments. This wave of economic stimulation rippled through the city, buoying its financial prospects and fostering dreams of prosperity.

Moreover, the plant's mandate to produce a pesticide integral to India's Green Revolution positioned Bhopal at the heart of a national agricultural endeavour. The city was not just fuelling its own economy, but contributing to a wider cause: the transformation of India's agricultural landscape. This sense of contributing to the national mission instilled a sense of pride and purpose among Bhopal's residents.

On the societal front, the factory had a profound impact. It brought together a diverse group of individuals, forging a sense of community and collective identity. It was an amalgamation of engineers from across the country, local workers seeking better livelihoods, and administrative staff managing the daily operations. They were no longer just residents of Bhopal; they were part of the Union Carbide family.

However, beneath this veneer of socio-economic prosperity, there lay hidden facets of reality that were far from rosy. The plant, with all its hazardous processes and materials, was situated perilously close to densely populated areas, a reality that exposed countless people to potential risks. Safety measures, while present, were inadequately implemented and communicated, thereby leaving the plant's neighbours uninformed and unprepared for potential disasters.

Additionally, the initial economic boom was slowly being undermined by cost-cutting measures and reductions in manpower. These cost-saving efforts compromised the safety standards of the plant, and over time, transformed it into a ticking time bomb.

The Union Carbide factory, therefore, had a dual socio-economic impact. On one hand, it boosted the local economy, created employment, and fostered a sense of community. On the other, it introduced a suite of hazards that were poorly understood, and even more poorly managed.

The irony is poignant: the factory that was once seen as a beacon of socio-economic prosperity became the epicentre of a calamity that would leave a lasting scar on the city's socio-economic fabric.

The City of Opportunity - Employment Boom and the Great Migration

AS BHOPAL CARVED ITS identity as an industrial hub, it exuded a magnetic pull, attracting hopeful individuals from

THE BHOPAL GAS TRAGEDY: UNRAVELING THE CATASTROPHE OF 1984

near and far. The city, with its burgeoning industries, beckoned scores of job seekers, leading to a dramatic surge in migration.

The Union Carbide factory played a pivotal role in this transformation. The plant, by its very nature, was a mammoth undertaking requiring a broad spectrum of skills and expertise. Engineers, chemists, skilled technicians, laborers, and administrative staff were all essential cogs in the machine that was the Union Carbide plant. As the plant's gates opened, so did hundreds of job opportunities, fulfilling the aspirations of many seeking employment.

The factory didn't just create jobs; it created careers. For engineers and chemists, it was a chance to work with cutting-edge technology in a globally affiliated enterprise. For laborers and technicians, it provided stable employment and an opportunity for upward mobility.

But the influence of the factory extended beyond the jobs it directly created. Like a stone thrown in a still pond, it caused ripples that spread across the socio-economic waters of Bhopal. Local businesses thrived, catering to the needs of the factory and its workers. From transport services to local food vendors, from housing landlords to small traders, the factory indirectly stimulated a host of business activities.

This economic boom led to an influx of migrants, not just from the surrounding rural regions, but also from far-flung areas of the country. Bhopal, with its promise of jobs and a burgeoning economy, became a beacon for those seeking a better life. The city's population swelled, and with it, the demand for housing, transportation, and other services.

However, this influx also brought with it a set of challenges. Many migrants, in their haste to seize opportunities, settled in hastily erected shantytowns around the factory. These settlements, often lacking in basic amenities, were alarmingly close to the plant. The inhabitants, driven by the dream of prosperity, were unknowingly exposing themselves to the plant's inherent risks.

Furthermore, the surge in population put pressure on the city's resources and infrastructure, leading to issues such as overcrowding, inadequate sanitation, and environmental degradation. Yet, these concerns often fell on deaf ears, as the promise of economic prosperity took precedence over these simmering issues.

The narrative of employment opportunities and migration to Bhopal is a study in contradictions. On one hand, it paints a picture of a city on the rise, a city of dreams where opportunities abound. On the other hand, it highlights the unseen pitfalls of rapid industrialization and unchecked migration.

THE BHOPAL GAS TRAGEDY: UNRAVELING THE CATASTROPHE OF 1984

Chapter 2: The Union Carbide Pesticide Plant

The Anatomy of the Pesticide – A Look into the Manufacturing Process

The manufacturing of pesticides, particularly the one produced by Union Carbide India Limited, involves a complex and intriguing process, a tightly choreographed ballet of chemistry, engineering, and human endeavor. Central to this process at the Bhopal plant was the production of methyl isocyanate (MIC), a potent and volatile chemical that forms the active ingredient in Sevin, a carbaryl-based pesticide.

The production of Sevin at the Union Carbide factory involved several key steps. The process began with the production of a chemical known as alpha-naphthol. This was achieved through a series of chemical reactions, beginning with naphthalene, a basic raw material.

In the next step, alpha-naphthol was combined with methylamine to create methylcarbamoyl chloride, a process that required exact temperatures, correct reaction times, and precision handling due to the volatile nature of the chemicals involved.

The most critical step was the creation of MIC. Methylcarbamoyl chloride was combined with phosgene, another highly reactive and toxic chemical, to create methyl isocyanate. The production of MIC was fraught with risks, given the chemical's volatility and toxicity. Its handling and storage required strict adherence to safety protocols, including maintaining low temperatures and pressure within specified limits.

In the final step, MIC was combined with alpha-naphthol to produce Sevin. Again, this reaction needed careful control over temperature and pressure, as well as precise handling to ensure safety and product quality.

The plant also housed a series of gigantic storage tanks, including the notorious Tank 610, for storing MIC. These tanks were designed to store the MIC at low temperatures to maintain its stability. Any deviation from this norm could lead to a runaway reaction, the catastrophic potential of which would be tragically revealed in the ensuing disaster.

While this description simplifies the intricate and complex sequence of reactions involved, it is important to understand the delicate dance that was the manufacturing process. Each step was a carefully calculated manoeuvre, each reaction a potential point of risk. The operation of such a complex process required a deep understanding of chemistry, an unwavering commitment to safety, and an incessant vigilance that unfortunately proved to be lacking in the Union Carbide factory.

A Thin Veil of Safety - Measures and Protocols at the Plant

THE UNION CARBIDE PLANT in Bhopal, by the nature of its operation, was a veritable minefield of potential hazards. Handling toxic substances, conducting volatile chemical reactions, and storing dangerous compounds necessitated a robust and well-maintained safety infrastructure. However, as the events of December 1984 would tragically reveal, the reality of safety measures and protocols at the plant was far from this ideal.

On paper, the plant was equipped with an array of safety systems. Key among these were the MIC storage safety measures. MIC, being highly reactive and toxic, was stored in large tanks that were designed to maintain its temperature below 5 degrees Celsius, a prerequisite for its stable storage. Any significant rise in temperature could trigger a violent chemical reaction, turning the storage tanks into ticking time bombs.

To guard against this, a refrigeration system was in place to cool the MIC and maintain it in a liquid state. Additionally, a vent gas scrubber was installed to neutralize any escaping MIC gas, ensuring that no toxic gas could escape into the atmosphere. Further, a flare tower was designed to burn off any excess gas that couldn't be neutralized by the scrubber.

Besides these, there were measures for worker safety, including the provision of protective clothing, respirators, and regular drills to educate workers about emergency procedures. The plant also had alarm systems to alert staff and nearby residents in the event of a leak.

However, while these measures paint a reassuring picture of safety, the reality was distressingly different. A combination of poor maintenance, cost-cutting measures, and lack of adherence to safety protocols systematically undermined the plant's safety infrastructure.

The refrigeration unit for MIC storage, designed as a critical safety measure, was shut down months before the disaster as a part of cost-saving measures. The vent gas scrubber, another key safety system, was inadequately maintained and was not in operation on the fateful night. The flare tower, designed as a fail-safe, was out of service and couldn't be used to burn off the escaping gas.

Safety drills for workers were irregular, and protective gear was often lacking or inadequate. Furthermore, the plant's surrounding communities were never educated about potential hazards or emergency procedures in the event of a leak.

In essence, the safety measures and protocols at the Union Carbide plant, though seemingly comprehensive, were gravely compromised. This not only set the stage for the tragedy but also amplified its impact when it did occur.

In the Shadows of Prosperity – Workforce and Labor Conditions at the Factory

THE WORKFORCE AT THE Union Carbide plant, an eclectic mix of skilled professionals, technicians, and laborers,

THE BHOPAL GAS TRAGEDY: UNRAVELING THE CATASTROPHE OF 1984

was the lifeblood of the operations. Yet, as the narratives unfold, it becomes clear that the labor conditions in the plant were a far cry from the ideal.

Upon its inception, the plant provided well-paying, stable jobs for hundreds. Engineers, chemists, and technicians found rewarding careers in a globally-affiliated enterprise. Manual laborers, many of whom had migrated to Bhopal in search of better opportunities, found employment as machine operators, maintenance workers, and in other roles. The plant was more than just a source of livelihood; it was a community, a symbol of progress, and a beacon of hope.

However, as years passed and the initial euphoria faded, issues began to emerge. A shift towards profit maximization led to cost-cutting measures, which unfortunately translated into a gradual erosion of labor conditions. Staffing levels were reduced, stretching the workforce thin and increasing workloads. Workers were often asked to handle tasks outside their expertise, compromising safety and efficiency.

Moreover, inadequate investment in training left many workers ill-equipped to handle the complex and hazardous processes of pesticide production. The use of contractual workers, who received even less training and lower pay, exacerbated the issue.

Safety gear, an absolute necessity given the toxic and volatile substances handled in the plant, was often lacking or inadequate. Respirators, protective suits, and safety goggles were not always available, and even when they were, their quality was questionable.

Worse still, the workers were often in the dark about the hazardous nature of the substances they were dealing with. Methyl isocyanate, the deadly chemical that would play a central role in the disaster, was handled by workers who were not fully aware of its lethal potential.

The plant's medical facilities were insufficient to handle health issues arising from exposure to toxic chemicals. Long-term health impacts were seldom monitored, and even when workers fell ill, they were often not informed about the possible connection to their work.

What was once a source of pride and livelihood for hundreds had turned into a precarious place of work. The workers, integral to the plant's operations, found themselves caught in a precarious balance, where their daily bread was laced with potential hazards they barely understood.

THE BHOPAL GAS TRAGEDY: UNRAVELING THE CATASTROPHE OF 1984

Chapter 3: The Night of the Disaster

The Night That Shook Bhopal – December 2, 1984

The clock ticked towards midnight on December 2, 1984, a seemingly ordinary night in the city of Bhopal. Unbeknownst to its sleeping inhabitants, a deadly cloud was about to descend upon them, turning the city into a vast gas chamber.

The chain of events began in the pesticide plant of Union Carbide India Limited. Around 9:30 PM, a small volume of water had somehow entered the E610 tank containing over 40 tons of highly volatile methyl isocyanate (MIC). The entry of water into the MIC storage tank sparked a deadly chemical reaction, causing the temperature to skyrocket.

The safety systems, which should have jumped into action to neutralize the runaway reaction, failed one by one. The refrigeration unit that should have kept the MIC cool had been shut down months ago as a cost-saving measure. The vent gas scrubber, designed to neutralize escaping gas, was inadequate for the quantity of gas released and moreover, it was not even operational. The flare tower that could have burned off the escaping gas was under maintenance.

By midnight, the situation had escalated beyond control. The safety valve gave way to the pressure, and a plume of toxic

MIC gas, along with other reaction products, escaped into the cool night air. Carried by the wind, the deadly cloud of gas slowly descended upon the city, seeping into homes and neighborhoods.

The effects were immediate and horrifying. People awoke to a burning sensation in their eyes and lungs. Panic ensued as residents tried to flee, only to collapse in the streets, their bodies convulsing in the throes of the toxic assault. The weak, the young, and the elderly were the first to succumb, their bodies unable to fight off the poisonous invasion.

The ill-equipped local hospitals were soon overwhelmed by the influx of patients, struggling for breath, their eyes burning, bodies writhing in pain. Medical personnel, unfamiliar with the effects of MIC exposure, were at a loss as to how to treat the victims.

As dawn broke, the magnitude of the disaster became painfully clear. Thousands lay dead in the streets, homes, and hospitals. Countless others were injured, many severely, their lives irrevocably scarred by the toxic gas.

The Bhopal Gas Tragedy had unfolded in its full horror. What was supposed to be a bastion of industrial progress had turned into a site of one of the world's most dreadful industrial disasters.

The Invisible Enemy – The Initial Gas Leak and Its Effects on the Surrounding Community

ON THE NIGHT OF DECEMBER 2, 1984, an invisible foe began to seep from the Union Carbide India Limited plant into the unsuspecting city of Bhopal. In the early hours of December 3, the gas, methyl isocyanate (MIC), had begun to infiltrate the air, homes, and ultimately, the bodies of the city's inhabitants.

Bhopal, sleeping peacefully under the winter sky, woke to a nightmare. The first signs of the leak were a harsh, choking sensation in the throat and a burning sting in the eyes. Coughing and gasping for breath, people began to spill from their homes into the streets, their eyes watering, skin blistering, and bodies convulsing in agony. The neighborhoods surrounding the plant, including the shantytowns of Chhola, Kainchi Chhola, Risaldar Colony, and others, bore the brunt of the toxic cloud.

But the deadly cloud was no respecter of boundaries or statuses. It seeped indiscriminately into every home, from the shanties to the relatively more affluent households. The gas, heavier than air, stayed close to the ground, making it particularly lethal for children.

The scene that ensued was one of utter chaos and panic. Disoriented, terrified people ran through the streets, their screams piercing the night. Some collapsed where they stood, overcome by the noxious fumes. Others, in a desperate bid to escape, packed their families onto vehicles or simply fled on foot, often leaving behind their belongings and livestock.

The hospitals and clinics were quickly overwhelmed with patients gasping for breath, their eyes burning, bodies writhing in pain. Medical staff, unprepared and ill-equipped for such a disaster, scrambled to provide relief with limited resources and little knowledge of how to treat MIC poisoning.

But the damage inflicted by the MIC gas wasn't limited to the immediate symptoms. Many who initially survived the exposure soon succumbed to their injuries. Bodies began to pile up in the streets, in homes, and at hospitals. In the following days, as the true extent of the calamity came to light, the city found itself in the grip of a disaster of unprecedented scale.

The initial gas leak's effects on the surrounding community were both immediate and enduring. It left an indelible mark on the survivors and the city of Bhopal itself, forever altering its physical, social, and cultural fabric.

In the Eye of the Storm – Response from Local Authorities and Emergency Services

WHEN THE FIRST WAVE of the gas-induced panic and chaos hit the city of Bhopal on that fateful December night in 1984, the local authorities and emergency services were thrust into the midst of a disaster of unforeseen proportions.

THE BHOPAL GAS TRAGEDY: UNRAVELING THE CATASTROPHE OF 1984

Local law enforcement, fire departments, and health services were the first to respond. But they were quickly overwhelmed by the scale of the disaster and the sheer number of victims. Emergency personnel, woefully underprepared for a chemical disaster of this magnitude, found themselves grappling with a catastrophe that was unlike anything they had ever faced.

Hospitals and clinics throughout the city were inundated with patients suffering from a myriad of symptoms, ranging from burning eyes and respiratory distress to convulsions and unconsciousness. Medical personnel, unfamiliar with the toxic effects of MIC, struggled to provide treatment. The lack of knowledge about the chemical involved in the disaster, and the uncertainty about the appropriate treatment for exposure to it, further complicated their efforts.

Local authorities were initially bewildered by the scope of the crisis. However, they quickly mobilized to handle the situation to the best of their abilities. Emergency shelters were set up for those who had been evacuated or displaced from their homes. Food, water, and medical aid were distributed, although the efforts were hampered by the chaos and panic.

A state of emergency was declared in the city, and the army and other paramilitary forces were called in to assist with the rescue and relief operations. The enormity of the situation eventually led to the involvement of national and international aid agencies and governments.

While their efforts were commendable, the local authorities and emergency services were ill-equipped and ill-prepared to handle a disaster of this magnitude. This lack of preparation and the inadequacy of the immediate response exposed systemic flaws in the city's disaster management strategies.

In the aftermath of the tragedy, these inadequacies fueled criticism of both the Indian government and Union Carbide Corporation. Critics argued that neither had taken sufficient precautions to prevent such a disaster, nor had they adequately prepared to respond when it occurred.

THE BHOPAL GAS TRAGEDY: UNRAVELING THE CATASTROPHE OF 1984

Chapter 4: Escalating Chaos

The Poisonous Fog – Rapid Spread of Toxic Gas and its Impact on Nearby Neighborhoods

On the fateful night of December 3, 1984, Bhopal awoke to an enemy it could neither see nor fight. The toxic gas that leaked from the Union Carbide plant rapidly spread through the city, silently infiltrating the unsuspecting neighborhoods nearby. This chapter seeks to provide a detailed account of that horrifying night and the devastating impact it had on the communities surrounding the plant.

The neighborhoods in the immediate vicinity of the plant were the first to be hit. As the clock inched towards midnight, the first whiffs of the pungent, toxic gas - methyl isocyanate (MIC) - began to infiltrate these communities. The gas, heavier than air, spread rapidly along the ground and seeped into homes, forcing those within to emerge into the cold December night, their eyes streaming, lungs burning, and bodies convulsing in agony.

Jayaprakash Nagar, a densely populated slum right next to the plant, was among the hardest hit. Its residents, mostly factory workers and their families, bore the brunt of the toxic gas. In this and other nearby settlements, the gas left in its wake a scene of apocalyptic devastation. People staggered through the streets, some collapsing where they stood, while others succumbed within the confines of their own homes.

Communities further away from the plant - Krishna Nagar, Chola Kenchi, Shanker Nagar, among others - were not spared either. Carried by the wind, the toxic cloud crept stealthily into these neighborhoods, the sleeping inhabitants oblivious to the mortal danger. The inhabitants of these areas woke up choking, their throats burning, eyes stinging, and bodies overcome by unbearable pain. Panic ensued as people tried to flee, often without fully understanding what they were running from.

The gas also infiltrated more affluent neighborhoods such as TT Nagar and the areas around the Upper Lake. Its indiscriminate spread illustrated the cruel reality of the disaster - it did not distinguish between rich and poor, old and young, man and woman.

The MIC gas, with its insidious and rapid spread, caught the city of Bhopal off guard. Its immediate effects were catastrophic, but the long-term implications were equally devastating. The gas affected not only the health but also the social, economic, and psychological well-being of the survivors.

The Struggle for Breath – Panic, Confusion, and the Struggle for Survival

PANIC AND CONFUSION reigned as an invisible enemy descended upon the city. As the toxic cloud of methyl isocyanate (MIC) spread across neighborhoods, a desperate struggle for survival began.

THE BHOPAL GAS TRAGEDY: UNRAVELING THE CATASTROPHE OF 1984

The first signs of the disaster were subtle but swiftly escalated. The initial symptoms – a harsh, choking sensation in the throat, burning eyes, nausea – quickly gave way to more severe reactions. People began to cough violently, their bodies convulsed, they fell unconscious or, worse, they succumbed to the deadly gas right where they stood.

In the face of this insidious threat, Bhopal was engulfed in a pandemonium of fear and confusion. Residents poured out onto the streets, wrapped in shawls against the winter chill, their eyes wide with terror and incomprehension. Entire families, struggling for breath, ran in an aimless bid to escape the deadly cloud, not knowing where to go or what to do.

Panic-stricken parents, coughing and gasping, clutched their children and ran, only to stumble over others who had already fallen. The weak, elderly, and children were the most vulnerable. Many succumbed before they could even comprehend what was happening.

Even as people fled their homes, there was no escape from the suffocating cloud. The gas, heavier than air, had an insidious presence, creeping into every possible space. In a desperate struggle for survival, people covered their faces with wet clothes or climbed to rooftops, hoping to evade the low-lying gas. But it was a losing battle for many.

In the midst of this confusion, some individuals and community leaders stepped up, guiding people to higher grounds, arranging for vehicles to transport the affected to hospitals, or simply providing comfort and reassurance. But such acts of courage and leadership were few and far between in the face of the overwhelming disaster.

The hospitals were ill-equipped to handle such a crisis. Doctors and medical staff, unfamiliar with the effects of MIC, struggled to diagnose and treat the flood of victims. There was a shortage of beds, oxygen cylinders, and medicines, further escalating the sense of panic.

The Siege of Sickness – Overwhelmed Hospitals and Medical Facilities

AS THE FIRST RAYS OF the morning sun pierced the chilling darkness of December 3, 1984, Bhopal's hospitals and medical facilities were already under siege. The city's health infrastructure, unequipped and unprepared for a disaster of this magnitude, found itself facing a nightmare scenario.

Emergency rooms across the city were inundated with victims gasping for breath, their bodies convulsing, their eyes red and swollen from the toxic gas. Hospitals like the Hamidia Hospital, Bhopal's main government hospital, and the smaller, private clinics scattered across the city, quickly ran out of beds, forcing them to treat patients in hallways, lobbies, and even outside in the open.

Doctors, nurses, and other medical personnel, themselves affected by the leaking gas, worked tirelessly, attending to patients, many of whom were in critical condition. But the staff soon found themselves dealing with a catastrophic lack of

THE BHOPAL GAS TRAGEDY: UNRAVELING THE CATASTROPHE OF 1984

resources – from oxygen cylinders and vital medicines to basic medical equipment.

Moreover, they faced a more fundamental challenge – the lack of knowledge about the nature of the poison they were confronting. With the absence of clear information about the toxic gas, medical personnel were unsure about the right course of treatment for MIC exposure. The uncertainty, coupled with the sheer number of victims, hampered their efforts to provide effective relief.

Compounding the situation was the constant influx of new victims. Ambulances and makeshift emergency vehicles continuously arrived, unloading more gas-stricken people. Families of victims crowded hospital premises, pleading for help, their desperation and despair palpable in the air.

The city's health centers turned into battlefields, and medical personnel into soldiers, fighting an invisible enemy that had invaded the bodies of thousands. Their efforts, though heroic, were insufficient in the face of the overwhelming number of victims and the severity of their symptoms.

This chapter of the Bhopal Gas Tragedy laid bare the vulnerabilities of the city's healthcare system. The inadequate preparation, lack of resources, and insufficient information exacerbated the effects of the disaster, contributing to the high death toll and widespread suffering.

OLIVER LANCASTER

Chapter 5: The Aftermath

The Harvest of Death – Immediate Casualties and Injuries

The morning after the disaster, Bhopal awoke to a chilling spectacle of death and despair. The immediate casualties and injuries of the methyl isocyanate (MIC) leak were staggering, the scale of human loss was unprecedented, painting a grim picture of one of the world's worst industrial disasters.

Within hours of the gas leak, the city streets transformed into open-air mortuaries. Bodies lay scattered in the narrow lanes and broad thoroughfares, some collapsed mid-flight, others huddled inside homes or on doorsteps. By some estimates, the immediate death toll was around 2,000, but other sources suggest that the number could be closer to 3,000.

Many victims were found with froth oozing from their mouths, a telltale sign of pulmonary edema, one of the deadly effects of MIC exposure. Others were found with wide-eyed expressions of terror, their bodies rigid with convulsions. Infants, children, and the elderly were disproportionately affected, their bodies unable to resist the toxic assault.

In the hospitals, the toll kept rising. Despite the heroic efforts of medical staff, many patients succumbed to their injuries within hours or days of exposure. The bodies began to pile up faster than they could be dealt with, leading to heart-rending scenes at mortuaries and crematoriums.

But the horror was not limited to the death toll alone. The injuries inflicted by the MIC gas were equally horrendous. The immediate physical effects of exposure ranged from minor symptoms such as eye irritation and nausea to severe issues like blindness, respiratory failure, and neurological disorders.

Nearly half a million people were exposed to the gas, and a large percentage of them developed severe health problems. Respiratory complications were the most common, followed by eye disorders, neurological problems, and gastrointestinal issues. Many women reported menstrual problems and had complicated pregnancies leading to birth defects in their children.

The scale and severity of the immediate casualties and injuries revealed the true extent of the Bhopal Gas Tragedy. Yet, they were but the tip of the iceberg. The long-term consequences of the disaster, which would reveal themselves in the years to come, were even more terrifying.

Racing Against the Reaper - Attempts to Control and Contain the Gas Leak

IN THE GRIM TABLEAU of the Bhopal Gas Tragedy, the frantic efforts to control and contain the deadly MIC gas leak offer a tale of desperation, courage, and bitter lessons. This chapter aims to provide an in-depth look at these attempts and

THE BHOPAL GAS TRAGEDY: UNRAVELING THE CATASTROPHE OF 1984

the challenges faced by those who sought to stem the flow of death and destruction.

The initial response to the leak at the Union Carbide plant was marred by confusion and disbelief. Workers in the control room, bewildered by the readings on their monitors, scrambled to understand what was happening. When the reality of the situation dawned, the plant operators made the first attempts to curb the disaster.

One of the primary strategies was to direct the escaping MIC gas through a network of scrubbers - tall towers filled with caustic soda designed to neutralize the toxic gas. But the scrubbers failed to function effectively, mainly because they were not designed to handle such a large volume of gas. Moreover, due to maintenance work, they were only partially filled with caustic soda.

The next line of defense was the plant's flare tower, a tall chimney designed to burn off escaping gases. However, the flare system was disconnected for maintenance on that fateful night, rendering it useless.

The plant operators then resorted to spraying water on the leaking tank, in hopes of diluting the MIC gas and reducing its spread. But the water jets from the fire hydrants could not reach high enough to make a significant difference.

As the severity of the situation escalated, help was sought from outside the plant. The local fire department was called in, but their equipment was also insufficient to reach the top of the stack where the gas was escaping.

Efforts were made to evacuate the plant's personnel, but the gas had spread too quickly. Several workers on-site became victims of their own factory, incapacitated by the toxic gas before they could escape or help in the containment efforts.

Despite the tireless and courageous efforts of the plant operators and the local fire department, they were ill-prepared and ill-equipped to control or contain the gas leak effectively. The disaster was simply too overwhelming.

Beacon in the Dark – Emergency Relief Measures and Aid from Various Organizations

IN THE BLEAK AFTERMATH of the Bhopal Gas Tragedy, the emergency relief measures and aid from various organizations served as a beacon in the dark for the devastated city. These collective efforts, albeit fraught with challenges, reflected the spirit of humanity in a moment of unprecedented crisis.

The immediate relief effort saw local, state, and central government agencies, along with non-governmental organizations (NGOs), rally to provide assistance. Temporary shelters were set up to house the thousands displaced from their homes near the plant. Food, water, and essential supplies were distributed among the affected population.

In the medical field, the city's hospitals were at the forefront, grappling with the colossal task of treating the gas-exposed patients. Medical personnel worked around the clock, with

THE BHOPAL GAS TRAGEDY: UNRAVELING THE CATASTROPHE OF 1984

support from healthcare professionals across the country. Aid also came from international agencies like the World Health Organization (WHO) and Doctors Without Borders, providing much-needed medical expertise and supplies.

Volunteers poured into the city, including medical students, social workers, and common citizens moved by the plight of the victims. They helped manage crowds at hospitals, assisted in distributing relief supplies, and provided comfort and support to the traumatized victims.

Non-governmental organizations played a pivotal role in both immediate relief and long-term rehabilitation efforts. Groups like the Indian Red Cross Society, the Bhopal Group for Information and Action, and Sambhavna Trust set up clinics, provided healthcare services, and advocated for the rights of the survivors.

The central and state government announced compensation schemes for the victims and their families. However, the process of compensation would prove to be a long and contentious journey, fraught with legal battles and bureaucratic delays.

In the face of the catastrophe, the immediate relief measures undoubtedly saved lives and provided succor to the victims. However, they also highlighted the deficiencies in the disaster management infrastructure, leading to important lessons for the future.

The Bhopal Gas Tragedy forced a reevaluation of emergency preparedness measures, underscoring the importance of quick response teams, efficient coordination between agencies, and the necessity of effective communication during crises.

THE BHOPAL GAS TRAGEDY: UNRAVELING THE CATASTROPHE OF 1984

Chapter 6: Seeking Accountability

Unveiling the Truth – Investigation into the Causes of the Gas Leak

The aftermath of the Bhopal Gas Tragedy necessitated an exhaustive investigation into the causes of the gas leak. Unveiling the truth was not just about assigning blame, but also about learning crucial lessons to prevent such a catastrophe in the future.

A slew of inquiries and investigations were launched by various Indian and international bodies to uncover the reasons behind the disaster. The Indian government appointed the Varadarajan Committee to investigate the technical causes of the accident, while numerous other independent scientists, engineers, and journalists pursued their own investigations.

One of the main questions was why the methyl isocyanate (MIC) had reacted so violently that night. The primary conclusion was that water had entered Tank 610, which stored the MIC, leading to an exothermic reaction that resulted in the production of a large volume of gas.

But how did the water get there? Theories abounded. Some suggested it was due to a lack of proper maintenance and safety procedures. The maintenance work on the night of December 2 involved washing out pipes connected to the MIC tank, and it was suggested that water could have accidentally entered the tank during this process.

Another focal point of the investigation was the plant's safety systems – why did they fail so catastrophically? Investigators found that the safety measures, including the refrigeration system that was supposed to keep the MIC tank cool, the vent gas scrubber meant to neutralize any escaping gas, and the flare system designed to burn off the gases, were all either shut off, non-operational, or inadequately maintained.

Union Carbide Corporation (UCC), the parent company, claimed sabotage, suggesting that a disgruntled worker might have intentionally introduced water into the MIC tank. However, this theory was widely discredited due to lack of evidence and the coincidental failure of multiple safety systems.

The investigations painted a picture of systemic negligence, poor maintenance, and a disregard for safety regulations at the Bhopal plant. The warnings from previous minor incidents, involving leaks and injuries, had been ignored. The plant was operating under reduced staff and budget cuts which had resulted in lax safety protocols and faulty equipment.

The findings from these investigations led to significant changes in global industrial safety standards, especially concerning hazardous substances like MIC. But they also ignited debates over corporate responsibility, environmental justice, and regulatory oversight that continue to this day.

The Scales of Justice - Legal Actions and Public Outcry for Justice

THE DEVASTATION CAUSED by the Bhopal Gas Tragedy sparked a fierce and enduring demand for justice. This quest for accountability manifested in numerous legal battles, widespread protests, and a global outcry for corporate responsibility.

Immediately following the disaster, public outrage against Union Carbide Corporation (UCC), the parent company of UCIL, was palpable. The company was widely criticized for its lack of safety measures, negligence, and inadequate response to the crisis. The Indian government, too, faced backlash for its perceived failure to regulate foreign corporations and protect its citizens.

The government of India sued UCC in a U.S. court for $3.3 billion in damages. However, the U.S. court held that India was the more appropriate forum for the case, and the litigation was subsequently moved to Indian courts. In 1989, after years of legal wrangling, UCC and UCIL reached a settlement with the Indian government. UCC agreed to pay $470 million in compensation, a fraction of the original claim, and without admitting any liability.

The settlement was met with widespread protests from survivors and activists, who saw it as a gross injustice. Legal battles continued in both Indian and U.S. courts, seeking additional compensation and cleanup of the contaminated site. However, these efforts have been met with limited success.

Public outcry over the disaster and the quest for justice extended well beyond India's borders. International NGOs, activists, and media took up the cause, bringing global attention to the plight of Bhopal's victims. The disaster has since become a symbol of the fight against corporate negligence and environmental injustice.

Protests, often led by survivors, continue to this day. Every year on the anniversary of the disaster, demonstrations are held in Bhopal and around the world, demanding justice, adequate compensation, medical care, and site clean-up.

Yet, justice remains elusive. Despite the public outcry and numerous legal actions, none of the company officials responsible for the disaster have been convicted. The site of the Union Carbide plant has not been fully cleaned, continuing to pose health risks for Bhopal's residents.

The quest for justice in the wake of the Bhopal Gas Tragedy is a testament to the resilience of the survivors and the global community's commitment to holding corporations accountable. The struggle highlights the imperative need for robust regulations, stringent corporate responsibility, and the protection of human rights.

The Puppet Masters - Role of Union Carbide Corporation and Warren Anderson

THE BHOPAL GAS TRAGEDY is irrevocably linked to the Union Carbide Corporation (UCC) and its then Chairman

THE BHOPAL GAS TRAGEDY: UNRAVELING THE CATASTROPHE OF 1984

and CEO, Warren Anderson. The decisions they made, or failed to make, before and after the disaster, have profoundly shaped its narrative.

Founded in 1917, UCC was a global giant in the chemical industry by the 1980s. When it established the Bhopal plant in 1969, the move was seen as a welcome boost for local industrial growth. However, the systemic negligence and cost-cutting measures that characterized the operation of the plant were symptomatic of a profit-driven mindset that largely disregarded safety and environmental concerns.

Warren Anderson, who helmed UCC from 1982, personified this mindset. Under his leadership, UCC embarked on aggressive cost-cutting measures across its global operations. At the Bhopal plant, this translated into staff reductions, including in critical safety-related roles, and deferring essential maintenance work. The safety systems that should have prevented or at least mitigated the effects of the MIC leak were rendered largely ineffective due to these measures.

In the aftermath of the disaster, Anderson flew to Bhopal, where he was briefly arrested and then released on bail. On his return to the U.S., he became the face of the perceived corporate indifference and negligence that led to the tragedy. Despite the public outcry and multiple charges leveled against him by Indian courts, he never returned to India to face trial, and the U.S. government refused to extradite him.

UCC and Anderson's reactions post-disaster further fueled the public outrage. UCC denied any wrongdoing and instead blamed sabotage by a rogue worker for the disaster - a theory that was widely discredited. Anderson, in a 1986 interview, showed little remorse or acknowledgement of the company's role in the tragedy, stating that UCC lived by "very high" safety standards.

In 2001, UCC was bought by Dow Chemical Company, which refused to assume liabilities related to the Bhopal disaster, insisting that the 1989 settlement resolved all claims. This further complicated the legal pursuit of justice for the victims.

THE BHOPAL GAS TRAGEDY: UNRAVELING THE CATASTROPHE OF 1984

Chapter 7: The Human Toll

The Survivors' Tale - Stories of Experience and Endurance

No account of the Bhopal Gas Tragedy can be complete without the narratives of its survivors. Their harrowing experiences, resilience, and enduring fight for justice offer an intimate lens into the human cost of the disaster.

One such survivor was Rashida Bi. A young mother at the time of the disaster, Rashida lost six members of her family to the gas leak. Over the years, she has battled numerous health complications, like so many others exposed to the toxic gas. Yet, her spirit remains unbroken. As a co-founder of the Bhopal Gas Peedit Mahila Stationery Karamchari Sangh, a union of women survivors, she has been at the forefront of the fight for justice.

Then, there is Champa Devi Shukla, who lost her husband to the gas leak. Despite her grief, she organized women in her community to demand healthcare and compensation, later receiving the Goldman Environmental Prize for her activism.

Satinath Sarangi, a metallurgical engineer visiting Bhopal at the time of the disaster, cancelled his return ticket and chose to stay. Known as "Sathyu" to the locals, he has spent decades working with survivors, providing healthcare through the Sambhavna Trust Clinic, and advocating for their rights.

Tales of personal horror abound. Babulal Gaur, who later became a minister in Madhya Pradesh, witnessed the nightmare firsthand, as people fled their homes, "coughing, their eyes watering, bodies convulsing...people vomiting uncontrollably, dropping dead."

Children born to survivors in the years following the disaster have not been spared either. Many suffer from serious birth defects and developmental issues, becoming second-generation victims of the catastrophe.

These stories of survival underscore the lasting impact of the Bhopal disaster. Yet, they also highlight the remarkable resilience of the human spirit. The survivors' relentless fight for justice, their refusal to be silenced, and their ongoing efforts to rebuild their lives in the shadow of such a cataclysmic event is nothing short of inspirational.

The Lingering Shadow - Long-term Health Effects on the Affected Population

THE BHOPAL GAS TRAGEDY was not just an incident that ended with the dawn of December 3, 1984. For the people of Bhopal, the aftermath has been a protracted saga of suffering, with the disaster's specter looming over their health for decades to follow.

The lethal gas that enveloped Bhopal that night was primarily composed of methyl isocyanate (MIC), but it also contained other potent chemicals. While the immediate impact led to thousands of deaths, the toxic exposure continued to inflict

THE BHOPAL GAS TRAGEDY: UNRAVELING THE CATASTROPHE OF 1984

damage long after the gas had dissipated. The health effects have been widespread and devastating, impacting survivors across generations.

Respiratory issues have been among the most common long-term health problems. Many survivors have chronic obstructive pulmonary diseases, asthma, and fibrosis. Eye problems, including persistent burning, tearing, and even blindness, have been prevalent due to the caustic nature of the gas.

The toxic exposure also wreaked havoc on the immune system of the survivors. There's been a marked increase in tuberculosis and other infections, and many have reported unusual and persistent skin disorders. Gastrointestinal disorders, such as stomach pain, chronic constipation, and indigestion, have become a common plight among the survivors.

Women suffered uniquely, with reports of menstrual irregularities, fertility issues, and an increase in pregnancy complications and miscarriages. The mental health toll has been immense too, with survivors grappling with post-traumatic stress disorder, anxiety, and depression.

Perhaps the most tragic consequence has been the impact on children - those who were exposed as infants or in utero, and those born to exposed parents in the years following the disaster. These second-generation victims exhibit a higher rate of congenital disorders, physical and mental developmental delays, and growth abnormalities.

Despite the multitude of health issues, the medical response has been fraught with challenges. Misdiagnosis, inappropriate treatments, and an inability to treat many chronic conditions effectively have added to the suffering. Efforts by organizations like Sambhavna Trust Clinic have sought to address these gaps, providing free medical care to survivors and conducting research on long-term health effects.

The long-term health effects of the Bhopal Gas Tragedy illuminate the far-reaching consequences of industrial disasters. They underscore the urgent need for strict regulations, robust healthcare systems, and effective remedial measures to mitigate such tragedies in the future.

The Silent Scars - Psychological and Social Impact on the Community

BEYOND THE IMMEDIATELY apparent physical health effects, the Bhopal Gas Tragedy inflicted deep psychological and social wounds on the affected community. These invisible scars have played a significant role in shaping the collective experience and memory of the disaster, profoundly affecting the social fabric of Bhopal.

Psychologically, the trauma of that fateful night has had enduring effects. Many survivors suffer from post-traumatic stress disorder (PTSD), characterized by flashbacks of the horrific event, nightmares, and severe anxiety. The chronic physical ailments and uncertainty about their long-term health have further amplified these mental health struggles. Depression and anxiety disorders are rampant among

THE BHOPAL GAS TRAGEDY: UNRAVELING THE CATASTROPHE OF 1984

survivors, often exacerbated by the loss of loved ones, livelihoods, and the struggle for justice.

The psychological toll has also extended to the second generation. Children born to survivors are marked by the collective trauma, with higher rates of mental health disorders, likely influenced by the chronic stress, grief, and health challenges experienced by their parents.

The disaster has also inflicted profound social impacts. The catastrophe and its aftermath have altered the city's social landscape, exacerbating social inequalities, especially among the poor and marginalized who bore the brunt of the disaster.

The gas leak led to significant loss of livelihoods, pushing many families into abject poverty. The long-term health effects often rendered survivors unable to work, leading to financial distress and social marginalization. The tragedy created a class of 'gas victims' – a social category defined by suffering and stigmatization, further marginalizing them.

The adverse effects on reproductive health resulted in stigma for many women, who faced social ostracization due to infertility, miscarriages, or having children with health issues and birth defects. The struggle for justice, compensation, and accountability became a common narrative binding the community, but it also served as a constant reminder of the disaster, reinforcing their 'victim' status.

Yet, in the face of these overwhelming challenges, the community has shown remarkable resilience and solidarity. Local organizations, often spearheaded by survivors, have emerged to support the victims, advocate for their rights, and provide social, medical, and psychological support.

The psychological and social impacts of the Bhopal Gas Tragedy are as significant as the physical health effects. They underscore the need for comprehensive post-disaster interventions, addressing not just the physical, but also the mental and social wellbeing of the affected communities.

THE BHOPAL GAS TRAGEDY: UNRAVELING THE CATASTROPHE OF 1984

Chapter 8: Environmental Devastation

Wounded Nature - Damage to the Local Ecosystem and Water Sources

The Bhopal Gas Tragedy's ramifications extended far beyond its human toll, laying waste to the local environment and irreparably damaging the city's ecosystems. Among the silent sufferers were Bhopal's rich biodiversity and its vital water sources.

The lethal cloud of MIC that night did not discriminate between human and animal life. Thousands of livestock and stray animals were among the immediate casualties. Dead birds dropped from the sky, small mammals and insects littered the streets, marking an ecological disaster alongside the human one.

However, the enduring ecological impact lies in the contamination of soil and water sources. The plant, during its operation, had reportedly dumped hazardous waste in and around its premises. Post-disaster investigations revealed widespread soil contamination within the plant site and beyond, with heavy metals and toxic chemicals like mercury, lead, and volatile organic compounds found in alarmingly high concentrations.

The most pervasive environmental issue, however, has been the contamination of groundwater, the main water source for many local communities. Chemical waste was recklessly dumped in solar evaporation ponds, which leaked over time, seeping toxic waste into the ground and contaminating the groundwater. This turned a human disaster into an environmental one, impacting both the health and livelihoods of those depending on this water for their daily needs.

Even decades after the tragedy, safe water remains a critical issue for Bhopal's residents, especially in areas near the abandoned factory site. The toxic water has further infiltrated the food chain, contaminating crops irrigated with the polluted water and the milk of animals that grazed on such lands.

Efforts to clean the site have been complicated and slow, marred by legal disputes, financial constraints, and lack of political will. Despite the local and global outcry, the site remains contaminated, a haunting reminder of the disaster, and an ongoing source of environmental and health risks.

The ecological impact of the Bhopal Gas Tragedy highlights the devastating consequences of industrial negligence on the environment. It underscores the urgent need for stringent environmental regulations and effective disaster response mechanisms to prevent such ecological disasters in the future.

In Silence They Suffered - Effects on Flora

and Fauna

THE BHOPAL GAS TRAGEDY'S effects on the city's flora and fauna were immediate and devastating. The lethal gas wreaked havoc on the city's vibrant ecosystems, while the ensuing environmental contamination led to prolonged ecological harm.

The immediate aftermath of the disaster resembled an apocalyptic landscape. Lifeless animals and birds lay scattered across the city, and the plant life surrounding the Union Carbide factory was scorched by the toxic fumes. Thousands of animals, including cattle, dogs, and cats, perished in the disaster. Poultry birds dropped dead, and smaller creatures like insects, particularly bees and butterflies, vanished, leaving behind an eerie silence.

The flora in and around Bhopal suffered equally, if not more. The dense vegetation near the plant wilted almost instantaneously with the gas leak, turning a once lush, green area into a lifeless grey. Gardens and farmlands were rendered barren, and tree leaves turned yellow and fell off, a chilling visual testament to the toxicity that had blanketed the city.

But the long-term ecological impact of the disaster was even more insidious. The residual toxic chemicals in the soil, coupled with the contamination of groundwater, led to a slow poisoning of the local flora and fauna. Soil contamination has stunted plant growth and affected agricultural productivity, impacting both the ecosystem and local livelihoods.

Moreover, the polluted water has infiltrated the local food chain, causing a bioaccumulation of toxins in plants and animals. Fish in the local water bodies have shown deformities and decreased fertility, suggesting the profound impact of water contamination on aquatic life.

Bird populations, particularly those of migratory birds that used Bhopal's numerous lakes as stopovers, have dwindled. The reduced insect population, likely due to soil and water toxicity, has further disrupted the local food chain, leading to a decrease in bird and amphibian populations that rely on them for food.

While comprehensive studies on the long-term effects on the region's fauna are limited, anecdotal evidence suggests a decrease in local biodiversity. Genetic abnormalities in animals and higher mortality rates have been reported, especially in areas near the disaster site.

The effects of the Bhopal Gas Tragedy on the region's flora and fauna stand as a stark reminder of the ecological cost of industrial disasters. They call attention to the imperative for stronger environmental protections and more sustainable industrial practices.

Road to Recovery - Cleanup and Rehabilitation Efforts

THE PATH TO RECOVERY following the Bhopal Gas Tragedy has been long and fraught with numerous challenges. Cleanup and rehabilitation efforts, from immediate relief activities to long-term initiatives, have been an arduous journey

THE BHOPAL GAS TRAGEDY: UNRAVELING THE CATASTROPHE OF 1984

marked by resilience, solidarity, and persistent struggles for justice.

Immediately after the disaster, emergency services, local authorities, and ordinary citizens mobilized to provide first aid, makeshift shelters, and basic necessities for those affected. Aid flowed in from across India and the world, including medical supplies, financial aid, and a workforce of doctors, nurses, and volunteers. Local organizations and international NGOs collaborated to provide urgent medical and humanitarian assistance.

However, the scale and complexity of the disaster demanded more than immediate relief. In the long-term, medical rehabilitation became a priority. Hospitals and clinics, like the Bhopal Memorial Hospital and Research Centre and the Sambhavna Trust Clinic, have offered free treatment to gas victims over the years. But, given the varied and chronic health impacts, providing effective medical care remains an ongoing challenge.

Economic rehabilitation was another critical need. With many survivors unable to return to their jobs due to health issues, initiatives were undertaken to provide alternative livelihood options. Non-profits and survivor-led organizations have facilitated vocational training and the formation of cooperatives for the production of goods, from garments to stationery.

Environmental cleanup, especially of the plant site and contaminated water sources, has been a complex and contentious issue. Despite several proposals and pilot projects for detoxifying the site and treating the contaminated water, a comprehensive cleanup has not been achieved. The site, still owned by the state government, remains contaminated, and groundwater pollution continues to pose severe health risks.

The rehabilitation process has also involved psychological and social healing. Community spaces, counselling services, and mental health programs have been set up to help survivors cope with their traumatic experiences and chronic stress. However, these services are limited and mental health remains a significant, often unaddressed issue in the rehabilitation process.

Overall, cleanup and rehabilitation efforts have been slow and marred by numerous obstacles, from bureaucratic hurdles to lack of funding and legal challenges. Yet, they have also been marked by the resilience and tenacity of the survivors, local communities, and activists who have relentlessly strived for recovery, justice, and dignity in the wake of one of the world's worst industrial disasters.

THE BHOPAL GAS TRAGEDY: UNRAVELING THE CATASTROPHE OF 1984

Chapter 9: Corporate Responsibility and Compensation

Behind Closed Doors - Settlement Negotiations between Union Carbide and the Indian Government

The legal aftermath of the Bhopal Gas Tragedy was a complex web of litigations, negotiations, and settlements, involving the Indian government, Union Carbide Corporation (UCC), and the survivors. The culmination of these interactions was the controversial settlement reached in 1989.

The Indian government acted as the sole representative for victims in a series of legal actions. In 1985, it enacted the Bhopal Gas Leak Disaster Act, granting itself the exclusive right to represent all affected parties, essentially centralizing the lawsuits filed by individual victims and associations.

The government filed a lawsuit in the U.S. seeking compensation of $3.3 billion from UCC, alleging negligence and breach of statutory duties. However, in May 1986, the U.S. District Court ruled that India was the appropriate forum for the case, citing considerations of 'practicality and convenience'.

Subsequently, the case moved to the Indian courts, where the government filed a claim for Rs. 3,900 crores (approximately $790 million at the time). Amidst these litigations, negotiations for an out-of-court settlement were initiated between the Indian government and UCC.

In February 1989, a settlement was reached, which was approved by the Supreme Court of India. UCC agreed to pay $470 million in full settlement of its liabilities, a sum drastically lower than the original claims. In return, all civil and criminal charges against UCC were to be dropped.

The settlement was justified on grounds of providing immediate relief to the victims. However, it was widely criticized as grossly inadequate, given the scale of the disaster and the ongoing suffering of the victims. Critics pointed out that the settlement amounted to an average of $500 per victim, a paltry sum for the catastrophic health, social and economic consequences they faced.

Furthermore, the settlement was reached without consulting the victims or their representatives, leading to protests and legal challenges. The opacity of the negotiation process added to the sense of injustice and dissatisfaction amongst the survivors.

Despite the settlement, the quest for justice continued, with renewed demands for higher compensation, cleaning up the contamination, and criminal liability against UCC. The settlement, seen by many as a miscarriage of justice, has kept the wounds of Bhopal fresh, fueling a persistent struggle for justice and accountability.

Band-Aids on Deep Wounds - Compensatory Measures for Victims and

Their Families

THE AFTERMATH OF THE Bhopal Gas Tragedy saw an urgent need for compensatory measures to address the devastating losses suffered by the victims and their families. Despite various efforts, these measures have been widely criticized as inadequate, delayed, and tangled in red tape.

The compensation came from two primary sources: the settlement fund of $470 million from Union Carbide, and the Government of India's disaster relief funds. However, the distribution of these funds proved to be a significant challenge, mired in bureaucratic delays and controversies.

A major issue was the classification of victims. The government classified victims into categories such as 'death', 'permanent disability', 'temporary disability', and 'minor injury', with each category entitled to a different compensation amount. However, due to the unprecedented nature of the disaster and the long-term health effects of the gas exposure, this categorization often failed to account for the actual suffering of the victims.

The process of claiming compensation was a daunting task for the survivors. They had to navigate a complex bureaucracy, provide extensive medical documentation, and wait for years to receive any compensation. In many cases, victims who were unable to document their injuries or those who developed health complications years later, were left out of the compensation process.

The compensation received by most victims was meager, ranging from a few hundred to a few thousand dollars. For many, this was woefully inadequate to cover long-term medical costs, let alone compensate for the loss of livelihoods and the suffering endured. Families of those who died faced their own set of challenges, as compensation was often held up due to issues related to legal heirship.

In addition to financial compensation, the government also provided other relief measures such as free medical care for the victims, job reservations for the kin of the deceased, and housing for those displaced by the disaster. However, the implementation of these measures has often been inconsistent and marked by complaints of inadequate facilities, corruption, and discrimination.

Despite these compensatory measures, many survivors continue to live in poverty and poor health, struggling to cope with the long-term impacts of the disaster. Their plight underscores the need for more substantial and efficient compensation mechanisms that account for the multi-faceted impact of such disasters.

The Price of Suffering - Public Perception of the Settlement and its Implications

THE SETTLEMENT BETWEEN Union Carbide and the Indian government was met with widespread criticism and protest, with many viewing it as a gross miscarriage of justice. Its implications have been profound, shaping the discourse on

THE BHOPAL GAS TRAGEDY: UNRAVELING THE CATASTROPHE OF 1984

corporate responsibility, legal accountability, and victim's rights in the aftermath of industrial disasters.

The primary grievance was that the settlement amount was woefully inadequate in the face of the disaster's magnitude. The sum, amounting to an average of $500 per victim, was seen as a pittance given the catastrophic health, socio-economic, and environmental impact of the gas leak.

Moreover, the process through which the settlement was reached was deemed opaque and exclusive. The victims and their representatives were not included in the negotiations, fostering a sense of disenfranchisement and mistrust. The settlement, seen by many as a top-down decision, failed to address the nuanced needs of the affected communities and left many victims feeling unheard and marginalized.

The decision to absolve Union Carbide and its officials of all criminal liability as part of the settlement was another point of contention. Many saw this as a denial of justice, reinforcing the perception of corporate impunity in the face of such disasters.

The public outcry over the settlement played a significant role in shaping the subsequent struggle for justice in Bhopal. It galvanized activists, non-profits, and the survivors themselves to continue their fight for adequate compensation, decontamination of the site, and legal accountability against Union Carbide and its officials.

The Bhopal settlement has had implications beyond the immediate case. It sparked a global debate on the ethical and legal responsibilities of multinational corporations operating in developing countries. The case has been used to advocate for stronger regulations on industrial safety, stricter liability laws for corporations, and more transparent and inclusive mechanisms for victim compensation in the aftermath of industrial disasters.

Despite the widespread condemnation of the settlement, it remains a poignant reminder of the daunting challenges in seeking justice for industrial disasters. It underscores the pressing need for global cooperation, stringent legal frameworks, and corporate accountability to prevent such tragedies and ensure justice for the victims.

Chapter 10: Rebuilding Lives

Picking up the Pieces - Rehabilitation Programs and Initiatives

Rehabilitation in the aftermath of the Bhopal Gas Tragedy involved a wide spectrum of programs and initiatives, designed to heal the wounds of the disaster, restore the social fabric, and enable survivors to rebuild their lives. These efforts spanned medical, economic, psychological, and environmental aspects, each carrying its own set of challenges and achievements.

Medical rehabilitation took center stage, given the wide range of health issues caused by the gas leak. The Madhya Pradesh government set up dedicated hospitals, like the Bhopal Memorial Hospital and Research Centre, for the treatment of gas victims. Various NGOs, such as the Sambhavna Trust, also established clinics providing free medical care. While these facilities have been instrumental in addressing the health needs of survivors, the sheer scale and complexity of the health issues posed ongoing challenges.

Economic rehabilitation was another critical area. With many survivors unable to resume their old jobs due to health problems, providing alternative livelihoods became vital. The government and NGOs initiated vocational training programs in fields like sewing, handicrafts, and small-scale industries. For instance, Chingari Trust, a survivor-led initiative, set up income-generating projects for women survivors. Such initiatives aimed to empower survivors economically and foster self-reliance.

Addressing the psychological trauma inflicted by the disaster was another crucial aspect of rehabilitation. Counseling services, mental health clinics, and community-based initiatives were set up to help survivors cope with their traumatic experiences. However, given the social stigma and lack of awareness around mental health in India, these services were often underutilized and insufficiently funded.

Environmental rehabilitation, especially the cleanup of the disaster site and decontamination of water sources, has been one of the most challenging areas. Despite various proposals and pilot projects, a comprehensive environmental rehabilitation has remained elusive.

Community rehabilitation was also integral to the recovery process. Initiatives like community centers, support groups, and cultural programs aimed to restore the social fabric, promote community solidarity, and provide survivors a platform to voice their experiences.

The road to rehabilitation following the Bhopal Gas Tragedy has been a long and arduous journey, marked by the resilience and tenacity of the survivors. While the efforts undertaken have made significant strides, the ongoing struggles of the survivors underscore the need for more comprehensive, inclusive, and sustainable rehabilitation strategies in the wake of such disasters.

The Healing Touch - Efforts to Provide Medical Care and Support to Victims

THE MEDICAL AFTERMATH of the Bhopal Gas Tragedy was a catastrophe on an unprecedented scale, with an acute health crisis unfolding alongside an uncertain path of chronic health complications. Providing medical care and support to the survivors was a colossal challenge, one that necessitated a multi-pronged, long-term approach.

Immediately after the disaster, local hospitals and clinics were overwhelmed with casualties. Doctors and medical staff worked around the clock, battling limited resources, a lack of knowledge about the gas's effects, and an influx of patients. International aid organizations, such as Médecins Sans Frontières and the Red Cross, provided emergency medical assistance, supplying much-needed medical supplies, personnel, and expertise.

In the long run, dedicated healthcare facilities were set up for the gas victims. One such institution is the Bhopal Memorial Hospital and Research Centre, a superspeciality hospital established by the Government of India. Providing free treatment to the victims and conducting research on gas-related diseases, this hospital has been a significant pillar of medical support.

The state government also initiated free treatment for gas victims at all government hospitals. However, this has often been marred by overcrowding, inadequate facilities, and a lack of specialists for treating gas-related ailments.

Several NGOs stepped in to fill the gaps in public healthcare. The Sambhavna Trust Clinic, founded in 1996, provides free medical care, combining modern medicine, Ayurveda (traditional Indian medicine), and yoga therapies. They also conduct crucial research on the long-term health impacts of the gas exposure.

Bhopal Gas Peedith Mahila Udyog Sangathan, a survivors' organization, has played a pivotal role in advocating for better healthcare for survivors, battling for medical insurance, proper documentation of health issues, and improved hospital facilities.

Psychological care has been an often overlooked aspect. Various NGOs, including Medico Friend Circle and the Indian Red Cross Society, have offered counseling and mental health support to help survivors cope with the trauma.

Overall, medical care for the Bhopal gas victims has been a journey fraught with struggles, victories, and lessons. It underscores the critical need for robust healthcare infrastructure, long-term planning, and holistic care to tackle such large-scale medical crises.

The Struggle to Reclaim Normalcy - Challenges Faced by Survivors in

Reintegrating into Society

IN THE AFTERMATH OF the Bhopal Gas Tragedy, survivors faced an uphill battle to regain their lost sense of normalcy. The disaster's impacts reached beyond physical health, dramatically altering their social, psychological, and economic landscapes, and the path to reintegration was fraught with numerous obstacles.

One of the primary challenges was dealing with the stigma associated with being a gas victim. This took many forms - from discrimination in finding employment or marriage prospects to the social isolation resulting from their physical and mental health issues. The stigma further compounded their emotional trauma, creating a significant barrier to social reintegration.

The disaster also resulted in a dramatic socio-economic shift. Many survivors, previously engaged in physically demanding jobs, found themselves incapacitated due to their health conditions. The loss of livelihoods, coupled with the meager compensation received, plunged many into a cycle of poverty. Reintegrating into a society that values economic productivity was a significant challenge for these survivors, necessitating alternative livelihood initiatives and financial support systems.

The physical and psychological trauma experienced by the survivors also created challenges in their personal and familial relationships. Families grappled with the emotional strain of caring for the sick, the grief of lost family members, and the stress of financial hardships. Many survivors also faced difficulties in resuming their roles as parents, spouses, or children, given their health issues and emotional distress.

For the younger generation, who were children or born in the aftermath of the disaster, the challenges were unique. Growing up with the tag of being a 'gas victim', coping with health issues, and living in the disaster's long shadow often had profound effects on their identity, aspirations, and social relationships.

Despite these challenges, the survivors of Bhopal have displayed remarkable resilience and tenacity. Through collective action, support groups, and rehabilitation programs, they have carved out spaces for themselves in society, reclaimed their narratives, and fought for their rights. Their struggles and triumphs underscore the importance of holistic and inclusive rehabilitation efforts that address the multi-faceted challenges faced by survivors in reintegrating into society.

THE BHOPAL GAS TRAGEDY: UNRAVELING THE CATASTROPHE OF 1984

Chapter 11: Activism and Social Change

Voices Rising from the Ashes - The Rise of Activist Movements and NGOs Advocating for Justice

In the wake of the Bhopal Gas Tragedy, a wave of activism emerged that took center stage in the pursuit of justice for the victims. A diverse array of activist groups, NGOs, and survivors' associations rose from the ashes of the disaster, orchestrating a powerful movement that has been integral to the Bhopal narrative.

These organizations came from diverse backgrounds and perspectives, but they were united by a common mission - to fight for justice, compensation, healthcare, and accountability in the aftermath of the disaster. Their work has spanned a broad spectrum, from grassroots activism and advocacy to legal battles and research initiatives.

Among the leading lights of this activism was the Bhopal Group for Information and Action (BGIA), a coalition of local and international organizations committed to seeking justice for the victims. BGIA has been instrumental in global advocacy efforts, conducting research into the disaster's long-term impacts, and pushing for corporate accountability.

OLIVER LANCASTER

The Bhopal Gas Peedith Mahila Udyog Sangathan (BGPMS), a women's collective of gas victims, emerged as a powerful voice in the fight for survivors' rights. This grassroots organization mobilized survivors, conducted public protests, and lobbied for better compensation, healthcare, and legal action against Union Carbide.

Another prominent organization is the Sambhavna Trust, which established a clinic providing free healthcare to gas victims and conducting critical research into the long-term health effects of the disaster.

Internationally, organizations like Greenpeace and Amnesty International amplified the voices of the Bhopal victims on the global stage, pushing for environmental remediation, corporate accountability, and human rights protection.

This wave of activism also impacted the legal landscape. Cases were filed in Indian and U.S. courts seeking compensation, decontamination of the site, and criminal charges against Union Carbide and its officials. While these legal battles have been long and arduous, they have been pivotal in keeping the quest for justice alive.

The rise of these activist movements and NGOs has been a testament to the power of collective action and resilience in the face of overwhelming adversity. Their tireless efforts have ensured that the Bhopal Gas Tragedy remains a poignant symbol of the struggle for justice, corporate accountability, and the rights of disaster victims.

THE BHOPAL GAS TRAGEDY: UNRAVELING THE CATASTROPHE OF 1984

Lessons in Ashes - The Impact of the Tragedy on Industrial Safety Regulations

THE BHOPAL GAS TRAGEDY served as a chilling wake-up call to the world about the potential hazards of industrial processes and the importance of stringent safety regulations. In its aftermath, significant changes were ushered in India's industrial safety landscape and spurred a global conversation on industrial hazards and corporate responsibility.

In India, the Bhopal disaster led to the enactment of the Environment (Protection) Act in 1986, a comprehensive legislation aimed at protecting and improving the environment. It granted the central government powers to implement measures for environmental protection, including the regulation of industrial activities.

Another key legislation was the Public Liability Insurance Act, 1991, which mandated industries to have insurance that could be used to provide relief to victims of accidents. This was aimed at ensuring immediate relief to victims, regardless of any legal proceedings.

Perhaps the most significant piece of legislation was the Factories (Amendment) Act, 1987, which introduced stricter safety measures for factories. This included more rigorous inspections, the appointment of safety officers in factories, and provisions for worker participation in safety management.

The disaster also led to the formation of the National Environment Appellate Authority in 1997, to adjudicate appeals against environmental clearances granted for setting up industrial projects.

Internationally, the Bhopal disaster spurred greater attention to industrial safety and corporate accountability. It prompted discussions on right-to-know laws, which mandate companies to disclose information about hazardous substances, and led to the strengthening of industrial safety regulations in many countries.

The tragedy also influenced the development of the 'Precautionary Principle' in environmental law, which advocates taking preventive action in the face of uncertainty and evaluating the wider environmental and social impacts before embarking on a particular course of action.

However, despite these regulatory changes, enforcement remains a critical challenge. Industrial accidents continue to occur, highlighting the need for more robust enforcement, corporate accountability, and workers' rights protection.

While the Bhopal Gas Tragedy has significantly shaped industrial safety regulations, it also underscores that the path to truly safe and sustainable industrialization is a continuous journey, requiring vigilance, commitment, and collective effort.

After the Smoke Clears - Lessons Learned and Changes Implemented Globally

THE BHOPAL GAS TRAGEDY, one of the worst industrial disasters in history, sent shockwaves across the globe and sparked a global rethinking of industrial safety, corporate

THE BHOPAL GAS TRAGEDY: UNRAVELING THE CATASTROPHE OF 1984

accountability, and disaster preparedness. The painful lessons from Bhopal have led to tangible changes and preventive measures being implemented around the world.

One of the crucial lessons learned from Bhopal was the importance of stringent industrial safety standards and regular safety audits. Post-Bhopal, several countries, including the United States and members of the European Union, bolstered their industrial safety regulations. The United States, for instance, passed the Emergency Planning and Community Right-to-Know Act (EPCRA) in 1986, aimed at helping communities plan for chemical emergencies.

The tragedy also underscored the importance of transparency and community right-to-know laws. The public's right to information about hazardous materials and risks in their communities became a major point of discussion. This led to greater emphasis on public disclosure norms and the creation of inventories of hazardous materials used by industries.

The concept of Corporate Social Responsibility (CSR) received a significant impetus in the aftermath of the tragedy. The incident highlighted the potential human and environmental cost of corporate negligence and put the spotlight on the ethical responsibilities of corporations. This led to increased scrutiny of corporate practices and a greater emphasis on CSR in corporate governance.

The Bhopal disaster also led to a stronger focus on disaster preparedness and response. Governments and organizations worldwide recognized the importance of having a robust emergency response mechanism to manage industrial accidents effectively. This resulted in improved disaster management policies and the establishment of rapid response teams.

Despite these changes, the Bhopal Gas Tragedy continues to serve as a grim reminder of the potential consequences of industrial negligence. It underscores the importance of continuous vigilance, enforcement of safety regulations, corporate accountability, and the rights of workers and communities. As we move towards an increasingly industrialized future, the lessons from Bhopal remain more relevant than ever.

THE BHOPAL GAS TRAGEDY: UNRAVELING THE CATASTROPHE OF 1984

Chapter 12: Legacy and Remembrance

From Tragedy to Remembrance - Commemorating the Bhopal Gas Tragedy

Even decades after the gas leak, the city of Bhopal remembers. Each year, as the clock strikes midnight on December 2nd, the city slips into a state of somber reflection. The Bhopal Gas Tragedy is not just a memory but a lived reality, a scar etched deeply into the city's consciousness.

The annual commemoration of the Bhopal Gas Tragedy serves multiple purposes. First and foremost, it is a time to remember the thousands of lives lost and affected by the disaster. Candlelight vigils are held at the site of the old Union Carbide factory, now transformed into a memorial. The flickering flames stand as a silent testament to the lives extinguished too soon.

The commemoration also serves as a platform for survivors and their families to share their stories, to remember and to heal. Public meetings are held where survivors recount their experiences, their struggles, and their resilience. These narratives are a stark reminder of the human cost of the disaster, a tribute to the indomitable spirit of the survivors.

In the city of Bhopal, the tragedy has been transformed into an enduring symbol of people's struggle for justice. The commemoration is marked by protests and rallies, demanding accountability, fair compensation, and decontamination of the site. These events serve as a powerful platform for the voices of the victims and activists, echoing their cries for justice that still resounds decades after the disaster.

Globally, the day is observed to raise awareness about industrial safety and corporate responsibility. Organizations, academics, and activists around the world host lectures, discussions, and campaigns highlighting the lessons from Bhopal and the ongoing struggles of its survivors.

Art and culture play a crucial role in the commemoration. Artists, writers, and filmmakers have immortalized the Bhopal tragedy in various forms, from murals and sculptures to plays, novels, and films. Through their works, they keep the memory of the disaster alive and provoke discourse on the issues it raises.

The Bhopal Gas Tragedy, while a grim reminder of one of the darkest chapters in industrial history, is also a symbol of human resilience and the fight for justice. Through their commemoration, the people of Bhopal ensure that the world does not forget, hoping that the echoes of Bhopal will inspire change and prevent such a catastrophe from recurring.

In the Shadow of the Catastrophe - Memorialization Efforts and Tribute to the Victims

IN THE HEART OF BHOPAL, a ghostly edifice stands as a stark reminder of the fateful night of December 2nd, 1984. The abandoned Union Carbide factory, an ominous symbol of the worst industrial disaster in history, has been transformed into a place of remembrance and tribute to the victims of the Bhopal Gas Tragedy.

The creation of the Bhopal Gas Tragedy Memorial was a significant step in honoring the memory of those lost in the disaster. This grim but important monument, erected near the disaster site, consists of a black stone wall with names inscribed of those who lost their lives. A mother and child sculpture at the center of the memorial serves as a poignant symbol of the many innocent lives claimed by the disaster.

Inside the factory premises, the abandoned machinery and structures have been preserved as a part of a museum to educate visitors about the catastrophe. Exhibits include photographs, newspaper clippings, personal artifacts, and survivor testimonials, each narrating a part of the Bhopal story. A haunting mural depicting the chaos and horror of the gas leak night serves as a stark reminder of the human suffering caused by the disaster.

But the memorialization efforts extend beyond physical monuments. There are numerous initiatives aimed at preserving the oral history of the disaster. Projects like the

"Remember Bhopal" oral history project collect and archive survivor stories, ensuring that their experiences, struggles, and resilience are not forgotten.

Every year, on the disaster's anniversary, various events are held to honor the victims. Candlelight vigils, moments of silence, prayer meetings, and artistic performances are organized by various community groups, NGOs, and activists.

The tribute to the victims also takes the form of persistent activism. The continued fight for justice, compensation, and remediation led by survivors' groups and NGOs is, in itself, a significant tribute to the victims. Their relentless pursuit of justice keeps the memory of the disaster alive and underlines the human cost of industrial negligence.

The memorialization efforts for the Bhopal Gas Tragedy serve a dual purpose. They are both a tribute to the victims and a constant reminder to the world about the catastrophic consequences of industrial negligence, inadequate safety standards, and the lack of corporate accountability. In remembering the victims of Bhopal, we commit ourselves to the fight for justice, the demand for corporate responsibility, and the need to prevent such disasters in the future.

A Battle Unfinished - Ongoing Struggles for Justice and Accountability

MORE THAN THREE DECADES after the Bhopal Gas Tragedy, the search for justice remains an unfinished journey. For the survivors and their families, the disaster is not a distant

THE BHOPAL GAS TRAGEDY: UNRAVELING THE CATASTROPHE OF 1984

memory but an ongoing struggle, a fight that continues against the backdrop of physical pain, psychological trauma, and social exclusion.

One of the main areas of contention has been the issue of compensation. While Union Carbide Corporation and the Indian government reached a settlement in 1989 for $470 million, many argue that it was woefully inadequate. The per capita compensation for the loss of life and health has been pitifully low, unable to cover the long-term medical expenses or provide a semblance of financial stability to the affected families.

The cleanup of the disaster site and the remediation of the contaminated environment is another longstanding issue. The abandoned Union Carbide factory is a grim reminder of the disaster, its soil and groundwater still contaminated with hazardous chemicals. Despite numerous pleas and protests by survivors and activists, comprehensive site remediation remains elusive.

Accountability for the disaster is perhaps the most contentious issue. Union Carbide Corporation and its officials, including former CEO Warren Anderson, have been accused of negligence leading to the disaster. However, attempts to extradite and prosecute them in Indian courts have been unsuccessful. In 2010, seven former employees of Union Carbide India Limited were convicted by an Indian court, but many see this as a mere drop in the ocean of justice.

Activists argue that Dow Chemical Company, which acquired Union Carbide Corporation in 2001, should assume responsibility for the disaster's aftermath. However, Dow has consistently refused to do so, stating that the liabilities were settled by the 1989 agreement. This has led to numerous protests and campaigns targeting Dow, including demands for their exclusion from events like the Olympics.

The struggle for justice has been marked by numerous legal battles, both in India and internationally. Cases have been filed for additional compensation, environmental remediation, and criminal charges against Union Carbide and Dow Chemical. While these battles have resulted in some victories, they have also faced numerous hurdles, including delays, jurisdictional issues, and enforcement challenges.

The ongoing struggle for justice in Bhopal is not just about the past; it is a fight for the present and the future. It is about acknowledging the long-term impact of the disaster, providing adequate compensation and healthcare to the survivors, cleaning up the environmental contamination, and holding corporations accountable for their actions. Above all, it is about ensuring that the lessons from Bhopal are not forgotten, so that such a disaster does not recur in the future.

THE BHOPAL GAS TRAGEDY: UNRAVELING THE CATASTROPHE OF 1984

Chapter 13: Health and Legal Implications

Echoes of the Past - Medical Research and Studies on Long-Term Effects of the Gas Exposure

The fallout from the Bhopal Gas Tragedy extends far beyond the immediate casualties. The large-scale exposure to toxic gases has had long-term health implications for the survivors and their descendants, creating a complex medical puzzle that researchers have been trying to piece together for decades.

Soon after the disaster, a flurry of health studies were launched to understand the medical consequences of the gas exposure. Initial symptoms included severe eye and lung injuries, skin problems, and neurological disorders. But as the years went on, the long-term effects started to surface. Chronic respiratory disorders, eye problems, neuropsychiatric disorders, and reproductive health issues were reported in unusually high numbers among the survivors.

One of the largest studies of the disaster's health effects was conducted by the Indian Council of Medical Research (ICMR). Over a period of 20 years, the ICMR carried out a series of studies that provided substantial evidence of the long-term health impacts of the gas exposure. These included a higher incidence of cancer and tuberculosis, various gynecological disorders, and genetic effects potentially leading to birth defects in the next generation.

International researchers have also contributed to the understanding of the disaster's health impacts. Studies have pointed to an increased prevalence of anxiety and depression among the survivors, a higher incidence of diabetes and hypertension, and the potential for genetic damage that could affect future generations.

In addition to physical health, researchers have also focused on the mental health impact of the disaster. Post-traumatic stress disorder, anxiety, and depression are common among the survivors. The disaster's psychological trauma, combined with the ongoing struggle for justice, has led to a high incidence of mental health disorders in the affected population.

Despite this extensive research, many challenges remain. A lack of comprehensive health data, discrepancies in health studies, and the complexity of distinguishing the gas exposure effects from other environmental and social factors have hindered a complete understanding of the disaster's health impacts.

Medical research on the Bhopal Gas Tragedy is not just about understanding the past; it has critical implications for the present and the future. It is crucial for providing appropriate healthcare to the survivors, understanding the potential health risks for future generations, and informing policies on industrial safety and disaster management.

THE BHOPAL GAS TRAGEDY: UNRAVELING THE CATASTROPHE OF 1984

The Fight for Justice - Legal Battles and Compensation Claims in the Aftermath

THE FIGHT FOR JUSTICE and compensation in the aftermath of the Bhopal Gas Tragedy is a saga of prolonged legal battles, fraught with frustration, hope, and an unwavering quest for accountability. Navigating the labyrinth of the legal system, victims, activists, and organizations have pushed relentlessly against the barriers, seeking redress for the cataclysmic disaster.

One of the first legal battles was against Union Carbide Corporation for compensation. After initial lawsuits were filed in the United States, the case was eventually transferred to Indian courts in 1986 on the grounds that India was the appropriate forum for the litigation. In 1989, the Indian Supreme Court approved a settlement agreement where Union Carbide agreed to pay $470 million in full settlement of all claims, rights, and liabilities related to the disaster.

This settlement, however, sparked a storm of controversy. Many criticized it as grossly inadequate, given the scale of human suffering and the long-term health impacts of the disaster. Subsequent legal battles sought to challenge the settlement, increase the compensation amount, and hold Union Carbide and its officials criminally liable.

Another series of lawsuits targeted the Dow Chemical Company, which acquired Union Carbide in 2001. Activists and survivors argued that Dow inherited Union Carbide's liabilities and hence should be held accountable for the disaster's aftermath. Despite these efforts, Dow has consistently denied these liabilities, maintaining that the 1989 settlement resolved all claims.

The compensation claims process itself has been a contentious issue. Although the settlement fund was intended to provide relief and rehabilitation to the victims, its distribution has been mired in delays, bureaucracy, and allegations of corruption. Many victims have received only a fraction of the compensation due to them, while others continue to battle in court for their claims to be recognized.

The legal battles extended beyond India's borders. In the United States, several lawsuits have been filed against Union Carbide and Dow Chemical, seeking damages for environmental contamination and demanding cleanup of the disaster site. However, jurisdictional and legal complexities have so far stymied these efforts.

The legal aftermath of the Bhopal Gas Tragedy serves as a stark illustration of the challenges in seeking corporate accountability for large-scale industrial disasters. Despite the numerous legal battles fought and the small victories won, many survivors still feel that true justice remains elusive. Their fight continues, fueled by the hope that their struggle will not only bring justice for Bhopal but will also deter future industrial calamities.

A Continuing Struggle - Litigation and Challenges Faced by Victims

THE LEGAL LANDSCAPE post the Bhopal Gas Tragedy has been fraught with twists, turns, and mountains that seem insurmountable. The path to justice is strewn with obstacles, making it an arduous journey for the victims of the tragedy.

A primary issue faced by victims is the complexity of the legal process itself. The bureaucratic red tape, the slow-moving wheels of the justice system, and the lack of resources often leave victims feeling powerless. Many survivors, grappling with health issues, poverty, and lack of education, find it challenging to navigate this labyrinthine legal system.

Another significant issue is the question of legal jurisdiction. Many of the lawsuits filed against Union Carbide Corporation and Dow Chemical have been mired in jurisdictional disputes. The complex interplay of national and international law has often served to delay proceedings and, in some cases, has provided an escape route for the corporations involved.

Then there is the question of corporate responsibility. Union Carbide and Dow Chemical have long contested their accountability, creating legal roadblocks that have been challenging to overcome. The corporations have leveraged their vast resources to fight legal battles, often leaving victims and activists feeling like David against Goliath.

Even when judgments have been passed in favor of the victims, implementing these verdicts has proved problematic. Enforcing judgments and ensuring compensation often gets caught up in legal and bureaucratic hurdles, delaying the much-needed relief for victims.

For those who have received compensation, another set of challenges emerges. The meager amounts, when distributed, often fail to cover long-term medical costs, let alone provide for a secure future. Moreover, the process of disbursing compensation has been riddled with corruption and inefficiencies, leading to further victim distress.

The litigation in the aftermath of the Bhopal Gas Tragedy highlights the chasm between justice and the victims of industrial disasters. It underscores the need for robust international legal mechanisms to hold multinational corporations accountable for their actions and ensure swift and adequate relief for victims.

The struggle continues for the survivors of the Bhopal Gas Tragedy, their fight far from over. Yet, they soldier on, their spirit unbowed, their demand for justice as urgent as it was over three decades ago.

THE BHOPAL GAS TRAGEDY: UNRAVELING THE CATASTROPHE OF 1984

Chapter 14: Global Industrial Safety Standards

A World Awakened - Examination of Industrial Safety Regulations Worldwide

The Bhopal Gas Tragedy was a catastrophic awakening for the world. It forced a critical examination of industrial safety regulations globally, underlining the dire need for their stringent implementation, constant review, and the need for accountability in the event of their breach.

Post the disaster, many nations tightened their regulations on hazardous industries. The European Union, for instance, adopted the Seveso II Directive, aimed at preventing and controlling major accidents involving dangerous substances. The United States passed the Emergency Planning and Community Right-to-Know Act in 1986, encouraging state and local authorities to develop emergency response plans and increasing public access to information about chemical hazards in their communities.

Developing countries, too, stepped up their safety regulations. India, the epicenter of the tragedy, passed a series of laws aimed at improving industrial safety. The Environment Protection Act of 1986, the Public Liability Insurance Act of 1991, and the National Environment Tribunal Act of 1995 were all designed to prevent industrial disasters and provide swift and adequate compensation to victims.

However, the implementation of these laws has often been challenging. In countries with burgeoning industries, inadequate resources, and rampant corruption, enforcement of safety regulations often falls short. Furthermore, multinational corporations, with their vast resources, sometimes find ways to circumvent these laws or leverage gaps in the legal framework to their advantage.

In the era of globalization, the issue of industrial safety has transcended national boundaries, becoming a matter of global concern. The cross-border nature of many corporations and the international trade in hazardous substances have made industrial safety a complex, global issue.

Many organizations and activists are now calling for a legally binding international treaty on corporate accountability to prevent future Bhopal-like disasters. This treaty would ideally have mechanisms for enforcing safety standards, ensuring corporate accountability, and providing timely and adequate compensation for victims.

The Bhopal Gas Tragedy has left an indelible imprint on the global conscience. Its lessons have spurred reforms and have been instrumental in shaping industrial safety regulations worldwide. However, the journey towards a safer industrial world is ongoing, with the echoes of Bhopal serving as a grim reminder of the road still to be traversed.

Ripples of Change - The Impact of the Bhopal Gas Tragedy on Industrial Practices

THE BHOPAL GAS TRAGEDY has undeniably left a lasting impact on industrial practices across the globe. Its ripple effect has reached far beyond the borders of India, serving as a grim reminder of the potential consequences of neglecting safety protocols and ignoring the rights and welfare of workers and surrounding communities.

One of the most significant changes the disaster instigated was an increased focus on safety. Industries dealing with hazardous materials now typically prioritize safety protocols and disaster management planning. Many companies have invested heavily in safety equipment, regular safety drills, and employee training programs to handle potential emergencies. Companies have also strived to incorporate risk assessments and hazard analysis into their regular operations, considering these critical aspects of their safety protocols.

Transparency and corporate responsibility have been another significant area of change. The disaster emphasized the importance of corporations being transparent about their operations, particularly those involving hazardous substances. This push for transparency has led to stringent regulations requiring industries to disclose information about the chemicals they use, their potential risks, and the measures taken to mitigate these risks.

The tragedy also highlighted the importance of emergency preparedness. Many companies have since developed comprehensive emergency response plans, coordinating with local authorities and communities to ensure swift and effective action in the event of a disaster.

Another aspect that has seen a change is the engagement with local communities. There is now a greater acknowledgment of the need for industries to work in harmony with their surrounding communities. Companies are now more likely to conduct environmental impact assessments and set up grievance redressal mechanisms to address any potential concerns from the local populace.

Furthermore, the disaster has also played a crucial role in shaping the discourse on corporate accountability. The aftermath of the tragedy exposed the challenges in holding multinational corporations liable for disasters, leading to a growing demand for binding international laws that ensure corporate responsibility.

Despite these changes, challenges remain. Not all industries have fully embraced these shifts, and enforcement of regulations can be lax in some regions. However, the lessons from the Bhopal Gas Tragedy have undoubtedly led to a more cautious and responsible approach to industrial safety globally.

Guarding the Future - Efforts to Prevent Similar Incidents

THE BHOPAL GAS TRAGEDY stands as a poignant reminder of the potential devastation that industrial accidents can wreak. It has sparked a global commitment to prevent similar incidents in the future, a dedication that has manifested in numerous strategies and initiatives.

One of the primary responses has been a tightening of regulations and laws surrounding industrial safety. Governments across the globe have made concerted efforts to formulate stricter laws, enforce compliance, and enhance the punishment for violations. The goal has been to make the cost of ignoring safety protocols too high to consider.

Technological advancements have also played a significant role in preventing future disasters. Innovation has led to the development of safer methods of production, storage, and disposal of hazardous substances. Furthermore, advanced monitoring systems have been devised to detect early signs of potential disasters, thereby allowing for timely interventions.

Education and training have been a cornerstone of these preventative efforts. Workers in industries handling hazardous substances now undergo rigorous training to understand safety procedures, the use of safety equipment, and emergency response protocols. The emphasis on safety education extends beyond the workers, with local communities also being educated about potential hazards and appropriate responses to emergencies.

Enhanced disaster management practices are another critical aspect of these efforts. Industries are now required to develop comprehensive disaster management plans detailing the strategies for handling emergencies, mitigating damage, and ensuring swift recovery. Regular drills are conducted to ensure that these plans are effectively implemented when required.

Public participation and transparency have also been encouraged to ensure that industries are held accountable. Public disclosure of information related to potential hazards, safety measures in place, and the response strategies to potential disasters is now often mandated by law. This public oversight serves as an additional check on industries.

Despite these efforts, the specter of Bhopal serves as a constant reminder that more needs to be done. The need for stringent international laws to hold multinational corporations accountable, the demand for better resources to monitor and enforce compliance with safety regulations, and the necessity for continual vigilance remain crucial aspects of the ongoing struggle to prevent a recurrence of such a disaster.

THE BHOPAL GAS TRAGEDY: UNRAVELING THE CATASTROPHE OF 1984

Chapter 15: Lessons for Corporate Responsibility

The Crossroads of Ethics and Accountability - An Analysis of Corporate Behavior

The Bhopal Gas Tragedy, with its profound human and environmental impact, starkly illustrates the critical need for corporate accountability and a rigorous adherence to ethical standards in the world of business. Its examination reveals two interrelated themes: the role of corporations in society and their responsibility towards various stakeholders.

Corporations wield immense power, often operating across multiple countries and affecting millions of lives. They have the capacity to bring about economic prosperity, generate employment, and drive innovation. However, with this power comes responsibility - a duty to protect and respect the rights of all stakeholders, including employees, consumers, communities, and the environment.

The tragedy in Bhopal underscores what can happen when this responsibility is shirked or overlooked. Union Carbide India Limited (UCIL) and its parent company, Union Carbide Corporation (UCC), were alleged to have ignored several safety protocols and standards, a decision that had devastating repercussions. This tragedy highlights the catastrophic consequences of prioritizing profits over people and the environment.

One key lesson from Bhopal is the critical importance of transparency. Companies must be clear about their operations, particularly when they involve hazardous substances or potentially harmful processes. In Bhopal, the lack of information about the chemicals being used and their potential effects hindered the initial emergency response and subsequent medical treatment. This absence of transparency was not only unethical but also led to higher casualties and long-term suffering.

Corporate accountability is another key theme that emerges from the tragedy. In the aftermath of the disaster, UCC and its officials, including then CEO Warren Anderson, were charged with various offenses by the Indian authorities, but extradition attempts were unsuccessful. The difficulties encountered in holding UCC and its executives accountable demonstrate the challenges in enforcing corporate responsibility, especially when it involves multinational corporations operating across different legal jurisdictions.

Lastly, the Bhopal disaster underscores the need for a strong emphasis on corporate ethics. Ethical considerations must be integrated into business decision-making processes. This includes ensuring safe working conditions, minimizing environmental impact, treating local communities with respect, and responding appropriately in the face of disasters.

THE BHOPAL GAS TRAGEDY: UNRAVELING THE CATASTROPHE OF 1984

The Bhopal Gas Tragedy serves as a grim reminder of the potential human cost when corporations neglect their ethical and social responsibilities. It underscores the urgent need for robust mechanisms to ensure corporate accountability, improve transparency, and foster a culture of ethical decision-making in business.

Lessons in the Classroom - Case Studies on the Bhopal Gas Tragedy in Business Schools

THE BHOPAL GAS TRAGEDY, while a historical and environmental disaster, has also found a place in the realm of academia as a powerful case study. Business schools around the world frequently examine the incident to extract important lessons on corporate social responsibility (CSR), business ethics, risk management, and crisis leadership.

In CSR and ethics classes, the tragedy is used to illustrate the importance of businesses being mindful of their societal and environmental impact. The disaster serves as a stark reminder of the potential consequences when companies ignore their responsibilities to stakeholders beyond their shareholders, such as employees, local communities, and the environment.

Students examine how Union Carbide's alleged lack of adherence to safety standards, failure to communicate the risk of its operations, and its response in the aftermath of the disaster all indicate a significant ethical breach. The case study underlines the necessity of prioritizing safety, transparency, and accountability, even in the face of financial pressures.

Risk management courses often use the Bhopal disaster to demonstrate the importance of having comprehensive risk assessment and disaster management strategies in place. The incident helps students understand the need for companies, particularly those dealing with hazardous materials, to proactively identify potential risks, develop contingency plans, and train their workforce to manage emergencies effectively.

The tragedy also provides valuable lessons in crisis leadership. The incident is often studied for the way Union Carbide handled the disaster—its immediate response, communication with the public and authorities, and its subsequent actions. Students critically analyze the company's response, drawing lessons on crisis communication, responsibility, and the role of leadership during and after a crisis.

Moreover, the incident is used in legal studies, examining the difficulties in holding a multinational corporation accountable for a disaster in another jurisdiction. It forms the basis for discussions on international corporate law, extradition treaties, and the legal responsibilities of parent companies.

The Bhopal Gas Tragedy case study serves as a pedagogical tool, allowing students to explore the complex interplay of ethics, corporate responsibility, risk management, and crisis leadership in a real-world context. It exemplifies the far-reaching consequences of corporate actions and decisions, ingraining in future business leaders the importance of conducting business responsibly.

Safety First - The Imperative of

THE BHOPAL GAS TRAGEDY: UNRAVELING THE CATASTROPHE OF 1984

Prioritizing Safety and Well-being in Industrial Operations

THE BHOPAL GAS TRAGEDY serves as a grim reminder of the absolute necessity of prioritizing safety and well-being in industrial operations. In the pursuit of economic gains, the well-being of employees, communities, and the environment should never be compromised. This chapter aims to underscore this critical imperative.

The Bhopal disaster was, in essence, a safety failure. A series of malfunctions, coupled with allegedly ignored safety protocols, led to the release of a lethal cloud of methyl isocyanate gas. The scale of the tragedy — thousands of lives lost, countless more impacted, and extensive environmental damage — illuminates the extreme consequences when safety measures are disregarded or inadequately implemented.

Industries handling hazardous substances carry an inherent risk, making the establishment and strict adherence to safety protocols crucial. Regular safety audits, maintenance of equipment, and proper handling and storage of hazardous substances are non-negotiable prerequisites.

Safety, however, extends beyond the factory walls. Industries must also consider the potential risks to surrounding communities. The tragedy in Bhopal demonstrated the devastating effects that industrial accidents can have on local populations. Today, industries are expected to carry out comprehensive risk assessments, considering not only the immediate workplace but also the broader environmental and societal impact.

In addition to physical safety measures, industries also have a responsibility to protect the well-being of their workforce. This includes ensuring reasonable working hours, fair wages, opportunities for career progression, and a work environment free from discrimination and harassment. A cared-for workforce is not just an ethical obligation, but also contributes to productivity and morale.

The Bhopal Gas Tragedy also underscored the importance of disaster preparedness and response. Companies must have detailed emergency response plans in place, covering evacuation procedures, medical response, and coordination with local authorities. Regular drills and worker training are critical to ensure that, in the event of an incident, an effective response can be swiftly enacted.

The tragedy has served as a wake-up call, prompting industries worldwide to review and enhance their safety standards. However, the commitment to safety and well-being in industrial operations must not waver. It is a continuous process, requiring vigilance, investment, and a genuine commitment to put human lives and the environment above profits.

THE BHOPAL GAS TRAGEDY: UNRAVELING THE CATASTROPHE OF 1984

Chapter 16: Media Coverage and Public Response

The Fourth Estate - Role of Media in the Bhopal Gas Tragedy

The role of the media in the Bhopal Gas Tragedy was both influential and multifaceted. As a critical source of information, the media played a central role in communicating the scale of the disaster to the global community, contributing to relief efforts, and amplifying the calls for justice in the years that followed.

In the immediate aftermath of the disaster, the media served as the primary conduit of information. Journalists and photographers braved the chaos and toxicity to report on the unfolding crisis, providing first-hand accounts of the tragedy. These initial reports and images, stark in their depiction of suffering and devastation, evoked global shock and sympathy. They brought the world's attention to Bhopal, galvanizing international aid and support.

As relief efforts began, media outlets served as critical platforms for disseminating information about the available aid and support services. They helped to coordinate the relief work, informing survivors about medical camps, food distribution points, and other essential services.

In the months and years following the tragedy, investigative journalism played a crucial role in uncovering the causes of the disaster and the alleged negligence of Union Carbide. Journalists dug into safety records, interviewed workers, and sifted through corporate documents. Their reports brought to light disturbing details about safety lapses at the plant, sparking outrage and prompting demands for accountability.

The media also amplified the voices of survivors, their stories of suffering, resilience, and their fight for justice. These narratives, communicated through print, television, and later digital media, kept the memory of the Bhopal tragedy alive, ensuring that it remained in the global consciousness. They also played a pivotal role in raising awareness about the long-term health and environmental consequences of the gas leak.

However, the role of the media was not without controversy. Some reports were criticized for being sensationalist or inaccurate, particularly in the chaotic early days of the disaster. There were also allegations that the media, particularly internationally, gradually lost interest in the Bhopal case as it dragged on over the years, contributing to the perceived lack of justice for the victims.

Overall, the Bhopal Gas Tragedy underscored the power of the media in shaping public understanding and opinion. It highlighted the media's role as a force for justice and accountability, and its responsibility in ensuring that the stories of survivors are heard and not forgotten.

United in Outrage - Public

THE BHOPAL GAS TRAGEDY: UNRAVELING THE CATASTROPHE OF 1984

Condemnation and International Solidarity Following the Bhopal Gas Tragedy

IN THE WAKE OF THE Bhopal Gas Tragedy, public outrage surged, not just in India, but globally. The scale of the disaster, the horrific human toll, and the allegations of negligence by Union Carbide stirred profound anger and demands for justice. At the same time, the tragedy spurred international solidarity, a unity of purpose and empathy across borders that offered support to the victims and their fight for redress.

The public outrage was fueled by multiple factors. Reports and images of the disaster, disseminated by the media, brought the harrowing details of the incident to global attention. The sheer scale of human suffering was shocking, evoking a strong emotional response. The tragedy was further compounded by allegations of corporate negligence, amplifying public anger against Union Carbide and its perceived disregard for safety.

Protests and demonstrations sprang up around the world. People from different walks of life rallied in support of the Bhopal victims, demanding accountability from Union Carbide and adequate compensation for the victims. Activist groups, students, workers' unions, and citizens took to the streets, holding placards, staging sit-ins, and organizing rallies.

This global outrage exerted significant pressure on Union Carbide, and indirectly, on the Indian and American governments. The intense public scrutiny arguably played a role in driving the subsequent legal actions against Union Carbide and its then CEO, Warren Anderson, and in pushing for the settlement negotiations.

The tragedy also spurred international solidarity. Financial aid, medical assistance, and other forms of support poured in from around the world. International non-governmental organizations (NGOs), such as Greenpeace and Amnesty International, took up the cause, drawing attention to the disaster's ongoing effects and advocating for justice for the victims.

Moreover, the Bhopal Gas Tragedy connected disparate struggles across the globe, forging a sense of unity among communities grappling with industrial hazards. The disaster became a symbol of the fight against corporate negligence, galvanizing environmental and labor movements worldwide.

Even as the years have passed, the Bhopal Gas Tragedy continues to evoke international solidarity. Commemorative events are held worldwide, ensuring that the memory of the disaster and the calls for justice remain alive.

The public outrage and international solidarity following the Bhopal Gas Tragedy illustrate the power of collective action in confronting corporate wrongdoing and championing the rights of victims. They remind us of our shared humanity and our collective responsibility to ensure such a catastrophe is never repeated.

Under the Lens - The Influence of Media

THE BHOPAL GAS TRAGEDY: UNRAVELING THE CATASTROPHE OF 1984

Coverage on Government and Corporate Actions

THE MEDIA'S ROLE IN the Bhopal Gas Tragedy extended beyond being a mere observer or reporter; it shaped narratives, influenced public opinion, and indirectly affected the actions of both the government and Union Carbide Corporation.

The media's rapid and comprehensive coverage of the disaster was instrumental in bringing global attention to Bhopal. The images and reports of the widespread devastation and human suffering were beamed worldwide, creating a sense of shock and urgency. They triggered an immediate humanitarian response, with aid pouring in from different parts of the globe. Both the Indian government and Union Carbide Corporation, finding themselves in the global spotlight, were compelled to act quickly.

The intense media scrutiny also pressured the Indian government to launch a thorough investigation into the disaster. The media's exposés of alleged safety lapses at the plant and the alleged negligence of Union Carbide drew public outrage, and the government was compelled to pursue legal action against the company.

Similarly, Union Carbide Corporation, under media scrutiny and facing a public relations disaster, was pushed into damage control mode. The company was pressured to respond to the allegations of negligence, the calls for accountability, and the demand for compensation for the victims. The intense media focus likely played a role in the company's decision to settle the case with the Indian government, though the settlement was later criticized as being inadequate.

As the media kept the memory of the Bhopal tragedy alive through their reports, it helped sustain public interest in the case. This ongoing coverage exerted continuous pressure on both Union Carbide and the Indian government to address the long-term consequences of the disaster and provide justice to the victims.

Moreover, the media played a significant role in highlighting the activism around the disaster, thus amplifying the voices of the survivors and various NGOs seeking justice. Their stories, struggles, and victories reached a global audience due to extensive media coverage.

However, it is important to note that while the media's role was influential, it was not always positive or accurate. In the chaotic aftermath of the disaster, some initial reports were inaccurate or sensationalized. Critics also argue that the media, particularly the international media, lost interest in the Bhopal case as the years passed, contributing to the perceived lack of justice for the victims.

Despite the criticisms, the role of the media in the Bhopal Gas Tragedy underscored its power to shape narratives and influence both public opinion and the actions of corporations and governments. The tragedy highlights the media's role as a watchdog, a purveyor of truth, and a driver of change.

Chapter 17: Governmental Response and Policy Changes

A State of Emergency - Review of the Indian Government's Response to the Bhopal Gas Tragedy

The response of the Indian government to the Bhopal Gas Tragedy is a complex and contentious topic, encompassing immediate relief efforts, long-term rehabilitation, legal proceedings, and settlement negotiations. While there were some commendable aspects, overall, the government's response has been widely criticized for its inadequacies and alleged failures.

In the immediate aftermath of the gas leak, the Indian government was confronted with an unprecedented crisis. With thousands dead and tens of thousands more affected, the government, both at the central and state level, sprang into action to manage the disaster. Medical aid was mobilized, temporary shelters were set up, and food and other essential supplies were distributed. While these actions were crucial, the scale of the disaster was overwhelming, and the initial response was criticized for being chaotic and insufficiently coordinated.

The government then initiated a comprehensive investigation into the disaster. The findings pointed towards several safety lapses and operational negligence on the part of Union

Carbide. Consequently, the government pursued legal action against Union Carbide and its then CEO, Warren Anderson.

However, the legal battle that ensued was a protracted one. The government initially demanded $3.3 billion in compensation from Union Carbide but eventually settled for $470 million in 1989, a sum criticized as woefully inadequate by many activists and survivors. The settlement also absolved Union Carbide of any future civil or criminal liability, which sparked public outrage.

Despite the settlement, the pursuit of justice did not end. The government continued to seek the extradition of Warren Anderson from the United States for his alleged culpability in the disaster. However, these efforts were unsuccessful, leading to further criticism of the government's inability to hold the key figures accountable.

In terms of long-term rehabilitation, the government established the Bhopal Gas Tragedy Relief and Rehabilitation Department to provide medical care, support, and compensation to the survivors. But these efforts have been marred by administrative inefficiencies, corruption, and accusations of inadequate medical support.

There were also allegations of lack of transparency in the distribution of the compensation amount among the victims. Many victims reported that they received only a fraction of the compensation due to them, leading to widespread discontent and allegations of corruption.

The cleanup of the contaminated site has been another area of criticism. Despite decades having passed since the disaster, the site is yet to be fully decontaminated, causing ongoing health and environmental issues.

Overall, while the Indian government did take critical actions in the wake of the disaster, its response to the Bhopal Gas Tragedy is largely viewed as insufficient and flawed. The tragedy exposed serious shortcomings in disaster management, legal recourse, and the protection of citizens' rights in the face of corporate negligence.

A Catalyst for Change - Amendments to Industrial Safety Laws and Regulations Following the Bhopal Gas Tragedy

THE BHOPAL GAS TRAGEDY sent shockwaves throughout the world, forcing countries to reassess and strengthen their industrial safety laws and regulations. It underscored the critical need for stricter safety standards, thorough monitoring systems, and greater corporate responsibility in hazardous industries.

In India, the tragedy led to significant changes in the country's legislative framework around industrial safety. Recognizing the inadequacies of existing laws, the government enacted the Environment Protection Act (EPA) in 1986. This comprehensive legislation aimed at protecting and improving the country's environment. It empowered the central government to take necessary measures to prevent, control, and abate environmental pollution, including setting standards for emissions and discharges of environmental pollutants from various sources.

Simultaneously, the Factories Act of 1948, which regulates the safety, health, and welfare of factory workers, was amended. The amendments strengthened the safety provisions related to hazardous processes, mandating stricter precautionary measures, regular health check-ups of workers, and the establishment of Site Appraisal Committees to scrutinize applications for establishing factories involving hazardous processes.

Moreover, the Public Liability Insurance Act was enacted in 1991, requiring industries to provide immediate relief to victims of accidents involving hazardous substances. This act was a direct response to the difficulties faced in providing immediate relief and compensation to the victims of the Bhopal disaster.

Internationally, the Bhopal Gas Tragedy had a considerable impact on the development of laws regarding industrial safety and the handling of hazardous materials. For instance, in the United States, the disaster influenced the passage of the Emergency Planning and Community Right-to-Know Act in 1986, part of the Superfund Amendments and Reauthorization Act. This law requires companies to disclose information about their storage of toxic chemicals and their release into the environment.

Furthermore, the tragedy sparked renewed discussions on corporate liability for industrial accidents and the need for international laws and regulations to hold multinational corporations accountable.

However, despite these legislative changes, there remains a continued debate about their effectiveness. While the laws on paper have strengthened, critics argue that enforcement remains a challenge due to resource constraints, lack of expertise, and corruption. There is also the question of whether these laws truly provide sufficient deterrents or whether more stringent regulations and stricter enforcement are required to prevent future disasters on the scale of the Bhopal tragedy.

Upholding the Law – Challenges in Enforcing and Monitoring Compliance Post-Bhopal

ENFORCING AND MONITORING compliance with industrial safety regulations is an ongoing challenge for governments worldwide. While the Bhopal Gas Tragedy resulted in significant changes to these regulations, several obstacles persist in ensuring their strict adherence.

One of the major challenges is resource constraints. Monitoring all industrial operations, especially in a country like India with its vast industrial landscape, requires substantial manpower, expertise, and financial resources. Regulating bodies often struggle with inadequate staffing, insufficient training, and limited budgets, making comprehensive oversight difficult.

A lack of technical expertise compounds this problem. Effective enforcement of industrial safety laws requires a deep understanding of complex industrial processes and the potential hazards associated with them. However, regulatory bodies often lack access to such specialized knowledge, making it hard to identify safety lapses or violations accurately.

Corruption is another significant issue, with instances of officials accepting bribes to overlook violations. This compromises the integrity of the regulatory system and allows negligent practices to continue unchecked.

Furthermore, in the case of multinational corporations, jurisdictional issues arise. These corporations often operate across multiple countries, each with its unique legal system and enforcement mechanisms. This can make it challenging to hold them accountable for safety lapses that occur in one jurisdiction but have ramifications in another.

Another challenge is the laxity of punishments for non-compliance. In many jurisdictions, penalties for violating safety regulations are relatively mild and do not serve as a sufficient deterrent. Some companies may consider these penalties as mere operational costs rather than severe consequences to be avoided.

The lack of transparency is a key issue too. Without clear information about the hazardous substances used in industrial processes and the safety measures in place, it is challenging for external parties to assess compliance. This lack of information also impacts the ability of communities to understand and respond to the risks they face.

Lastly, there is the problem of implementation. Even with robust laws in place, the practical application can falter due to unclear guidelines, bureaucratic red tape, and a lack of coordination among different governmental bodies.

Despite these challenges, it is crucial for regulatory bodies to enforce and monitor compliance with industrial safety laws strictly. The Bhopal Gas Tragedy underscores the catastrophic consequences of regulatory failure. Ensuring the effective enforcement of these laws is not just a legal necessity but a moral obligation to safeguard lives, livelihoods, and the environment.

OLIVER LANCASTER

Chapter 18: Unanswered Questions and Lingering Controversies

A Wound Yet to Heal - Unresolved Issues Surrounding the Bhopal Gas Tragedy

Despite the passage of nearly four decades, several critical issues surrounding the Bhopal Gas Tragedy remain unresolved, casting long shadows over the victims, the city of Bhopal, and the broader global community. These unresolved issues continue to provoke anger, fuel activism, and drive demands for justice and accountability.

One of the primary unresolved issues is the full and final cleanup of the disaster site. Tons of hazardous waste remain buried in the grounds of the former Union Carbide factory, slowly leaching into the local groundwater and posing a severe health risk to the nearby communities. Despite repeated calls from environmentalists and rights groups, a comprehensive cleanup operation is yet to be undertaken, largely due to disagreements over responsibility between the Indian government, the state government of Madhya Pradesh, and Dow Chemical Company, which took over Union Carbide in 2001.

Another critical issue is the incomplete disbursement of compensation to the victims and their families. While a $470 million settlement was reached with Union Carbide in 1989, there have been consistent complaints about the unfair distribution of these funds. Many victims claim to have received only a fraction of what they were entitled to, or nothing at all, due to bureaucratic inefficiencies and corruption.

The health effects of the gas leak continue to plague the survivors and their children. There is evidence of genetic damage and high rates of cancers and other serious illnesses among the survivors and their offspring. The victims have long demanded better healthcare facilities and more comprehensive medical research into the long-term effects of the disaster, but their demands have largely been unmet.

The quest for corporate accountability also remains a significant unresolved issue. Despite the evidence of safety lapses and operational negligence, Union Carbide and its then-CEO, Warren Anderson, were never held fully accountable for the disaster. Anderson's extradition from the United States was sought by the Indian government, but it was not granted, and he passed away without facing trial in India.

Lastly, the impact on the environment is a grim reminder of the tragedy. The region's flora and fauna have been drastically affected, with reports of soil and groundwater contamination affecting the growth of plants and health of animals.

These unresolved issues are a poignant reminder of the enduring aftermath of the Bhopal Gas Tragedy. They underline the continuing struggle for justice, recompense, and closure for one of the world's most horrific industrial disasters.

THE BHOPAL GAS TRAGEDY: UNRAVELING THE CATASTROPHE OF 1984

Shadows and Suspicions - Allegations of Government Cover-ups and Corporate Influence

IN THE AFTERMATH OF the Bhopal Gas Tragedy, accusations of government cover-ups and undue corporate influence have added another layer of complexity to the story. These allegations, sometimes rooted in confirmed facts and at other times in speculative suspicions, have fueled widespread public skepticism and mistrust.

One of the most contentious allegations revolves around the role of Union Carbide Corporation (UCC) and its CEO, Warren Anderson. The rapid and somewhat unexpected departure of Anderson from India shortly after the disaster, allegedly facilitated by high-ranking Indian officials, led to widespread speculation of a government cover-up. Critics argue that the government was overly lenient in its dealings with Anderson and UCC due to the influence of powerful corporate and diplomatic interests.

Furthermore, there is an ongoing controversy over the immediate cause of the gas leak. While it is widely accepted that poor maintenance and inadequate safety measures were key contributors, the exact sequence of events leading to the leak remains contentious. UCC maintains that the disaster was caused by sabotage by a disgruntled employee, a claim vehemently disputed by activists and survivors. Many view this stance as a corporate strategy to shift the blame and escape liability.

The settlement amount of $470 million agreed upon by the Indian government and UCC in 1989 is another point of contention. Critics argue that the government undersold the claim due to corporate and diplomatic pressure. Moreover, the lack of transparency and rampant corruption in the disbursement of compensation funds has raised further suspicions of government negligence and wrongdoing.

There are also allegations that both Union Carbide and the government suppressed or ignored early warnings of a possible disaster. Reports indicate that safety audits conducted by experts identified several serious safety hazards at the Bhopal plant, but no substantive corrective measures were implemented.

Finally, the handling of the disaster site cleanup has been fraught with allegations of cover-ups. The site, which still holds vast amounts of hazardous waste, has not been properly cleaned up, leading to ongoing environmental and health issues. Critics argue that both the government and Dow Chemical, which acquired Union Carbide, have evaded their responsibilities in this regard.

While the extent of truth behind these allegations varies, they nevertheless highlight the intertwined complexities of corporate accountability, political power, and justice in the aftermath of industrial disasters. These ongoing controversies continue to cast a long and troubling shadow over the legacy of the Bhopal Gas Tragedy.

Of Shadows and Whispers - Conspiracy

THE BHOPAL GAS TRAGEDY: UNRAVELING THE CATASTROPHE OF 1984

Theories and their Impact on Public Perception

IN THE WAKE OF SIGNIFICANT tragedies, conspiracy theories often proliferate. The Bhopal Gas Tragedy is no exception. The lack of transparency and perceived impunity of those responsible have spurred numerous conspiracy theories, which have deeply influenced public perception and attitudes towards the disaster.

Perhaps the most pervasive conspiracy theory is the suggestion that the gas leak was not an accident but a deliberate act of sabotage. This theory, initially proposed by Union Carbide itself as a defense, suggests that a disgruntled employee intentionally caused the leak. While there's no substantial evidence to support this theory, it has found a foothold in some circles, muddying the waters and redirecting blame from systemic operational and safety failings to an individual act.

Another prevalent theory revolves around the hasty departure of Union Carbide's CEO, Warren Anderson, from India. Many believe that this was facilitated by high-ranking officials in the Indian government in exchange for undisclosed favors or under diplomatic pressure from the United States. This theory fuels mistrust towards the government and reinforces the narrative of an unequal power dynamic between corporations and national authorities.

The surprisingly low settlement amount between Union Carbide and the Indian government has also generated considerable speculation. Critics suggest that the government deliberately undervalued the claim due to corporate pressure or diplomatic considerations, effectively selling out the victims. While not a conspiracy theory in the traditional sense, it underscores the prevalent perception of the government's failure to secure justice for the victims.

These conspiracy theories, regardless of their veracity, have had a substantial impact on public perception. They have fueled mistrust towards both the government and multinational corporations, stoking a sense of injustice and anger. Moreover, they have galvanized activism and demands for further investigations and legal actions against Union Carbide and its successors.

However, it's crucial to note that while these conspiracy theories offer tantalizing narratives, they often distract from the more pressing and substantiated issues, such as corporate negligence, inadequate safety regulations, and failure of oversight. These are the systemic failings that truly underpin the Bhopal disaster, and they require as much attention and scrutiny as the more speculative narratives.

THE BHOPAL GAS TRAGEDY: UNRAVELING THE CATASTROPHE OF 1984

Chapter 19: Bhopal Today: Reflections and Progress

Echoes of a Tragedy - The Current State of Bhopal and the Affected Communities

As we turn our gaze to the present day, the city of Bhopal and the communities affected by the gas leak continue to bear the scars of the disaster. The aftermath of the Bhopal Gas Tragedy has permeated every aspect of life, shaping the social, economic, environmental, and health landscape of the city.

The most noticeable impact is on the health of the survivors and their descendants. Despite being nearly four decades since the disaster, medical complications attributable to gas exposure persist. Chronic respiratory illnesses, eye problems, and an elevated rate of cancers are still prevalent among the survivors. Additionally, research suggests that the children of survivors have higher rates of birth defects and developmental disorders, indicating a transgenerational impact of the exposure.

In the shadow of the now-defunct Union Carbide plant, communities live with the constant reminder of the disaster. Many of the affected areas, particularly the bustees or slums adjacent to the plant, still suffer from contaminated water sources due to the improper disposal of hazardous waste. Despite numerous pleas for thorough cleanup and remediation, the task remains incomplete, leaving these communities in a constant state of health risk.

Economically, the disaster's legacy has had a mixed impact. On one hand, the attention and funding directed towards Bhopal following the tragedy have stimulated development and growth in some sectors. On the other hand, many survivors, especially those with chronic health issues, find it difficult to secure regular employment, pushing them into a cycle of poverty.

Socio-culturally, the tragedy has left a deep imprint on the communal psyche. The memory of the disaster continues to shape the identities of the survivors and their families, influencing their attitudes towards government, corporations, and notions of justice. The persistent struggle for justice and compensation has become a central part of life for many.

On a broader level, Bhopal has witnessed a rise in activism and advocacy. Numerous NGOs, like the Bhopal Group for Information and Action and the Sambhavna Trust, continue to fight for the rights of the survivors, seeking compensation, medical aid, and cleanup of the disaster site. This activism has also driven changes in local attitudes towards environmental sustainability and corporate responsibility.

Despite the significant strides made in the recovery process, the current state of Bhopal and the affected communities underlines the enduring and multifaceted impact of the Bhopal Gas Tragedy. The city's struggle with the aftermath of the disaster serves as a poignant reminder of the long-term effects of industrial disasters and the imperative of preventing such incidents in the future.

From Tragedy to Transformation - Efforts towards Economic Revitalization and Social Development

IN THE WAKE OF THE Bhopal Gas Tragedy, the journey to recovery has been a daunting task. However, through tireless efforts from various sectors, progress has been made towards economic revitalization and social development, transforming the narrative from one of tragedy to one of resilience and renewal.

Economic revitalization in Bhopal has been a multifaceted endeavor. With funding from the central and state government, and international organizations, Bhopal has undertaken significant infrastructural development projects. These have not only generated employment but also helped modernize the city. The establishment of the Bhopal Municipal Corporation's City Development Plan represents a comprehensive strategy to promote sustainable urban growth and economic diversification.

Further, Bhopal has seen significant growth in sectors like information technology, education, and healthcare. The establishment of institutions such as the All India Institute of Medical Sciences (AIIMS) Bhopal, Indian Institute of Science Education and Research (IISER) Bhopal, and software technology parks have been instrumental in this economic transformation.

Social development initiatives have also been crucial in the city's recovery process. These efforts range from healthcare initiatives and educational programs to livelihood training and community empowerment projects. Several NGOs have worked tirelessly to provide medical care, vocational training, legal aid, and psychological support to the survivors and their families. For instance, the Sambhavna Trust Clinic offers free medical care to survivors, and Chingari Trust provides rehabilitation to children born with physical and mental disabilities.

The Bhopal disaster also instigated a shift in the city's societal norms. The tragic event fostered a strong sense of community among survivors, leading to the rise of women's groups, neighborhood organizations, and advocacy networks. These groups have empowered the marginalized, fostered solidarity, and pushed for social justice.

The role of environmental restoration in Bhopal's revitalization cannot be understated. While the remediation of the disaster site remains incomplete, the city has made strides in other areas. For instance, the creation of Van Vihar National Park, a sprawling green space in the heart of Bhopal, signifies the city's commitment to environmental preservation.

In essence, the journey of Bhopal, post-disaster, has been one of determination and resilience. The city has gradually transitioned from a symbol of industrial catastrophe to a testament to recovery and transformation. Despite the many challenges that remain, these efforts towards economic revitalization and social development serve as a beacon of hope for the city and its inhabitants.

The Unfinished Journey – Continuing Challenges and the Fight for Justice

EVEN AS BHOPAL SLOWLY but surely recuperates and reinvents itself, numerous challenges still loom large over the city and its inhabitants, especially those directly affected by the tragedy. Four decades on, the fight for justice and adequate compensation continues to be a long-drawn struggle, laden with complexities and frustrations.

One of the most significant challenges lies in securing just compensation for the survivors and their families. While the settlement reached between Union Carbide and the Indian government provided some relief, it's widely regarded as woefully inadequate. Victims and advocacy groups argue that it fails to account for the true number of people affected or the long-term health implications of the disaster. The process of distributing the compensation has also been mired in red tape and corruption, leaving many victims still awaiting their due.

Medical treatment for the survivors presents another significant challenge. The long-term health effects of the gas exposure are still evident in the affected population, with many continuing to suffer from a plethora of ailments. The need for sustained medical research and specialized care for these individuals is immense, yet the resources are often lacking. Similarly, the mental health repercussions of the disaster – a lesser-acknowledged but equally important aspect – requires more attention and intervention.

The lingering environmental damage also constitutes a major obstacle. Despite numerous studies highlighting soil and groundwater contamination in and around the old Union Carbide plant, comprehensive cleanup and remediation efforts have yet to take place. This situation not only poses a continued health risk to nearby communities but also stands as a constant, grim reminder of the catastrophe.

On a broader level, the struggle for justice for the Bhopal Gas Tragedy survivors goes beyond compensation and cleanup. It's about corporate accountability and the responsibility that multinationals must bear for their actions. Despite the Indian government's attempts to extradite Union Carbide's CEO Warren Anderson, he died without facing trial, adding to the sense of injustice felt by many.

The fight for justice is carried forward by survivors, their families, and numerous advocacy groups who refuse to let the world forget about Bhopal. Through protests, public education campaigns, legal battles, and lobbying, they continue to demand accountability, fair compensation, medical care, and environmental cleanup. This collective action keeps the memory of the Bhopal Gas Tragedy alive and underscores the crucial need for corporate responsibility and stringent safety measures in industries worldwide.

Though challenges persist, the strength and resilience of the Bhopal survivors and their relentless quest for justice underline

THE BHOPAL GAS TRAGEDY: UNRAVELING THE CATASTROPHE OF 1984

a critical message: the story of Bhopal is far from over, and their fight is our fight too.

OLIVER LANCASTER

Epilogue: Remembering Bhopal

Remembering Bhopal - Final Thoughts on the Enduring Legacy

The Bhopal Gas Tragedy stands as an indelible mark on human history, forever etched in the memories of those who lived through it and the generations that followed. Its enduring legacy extends far beyond the immediate devastation and encompasses a multitude of complex issues and lessons that continue to resonate today.

First and foremost, the tragedy serves as a stark reminder of the devastating consequences of industrial negligence. It exposes the vulnerability of communities living in the shadows of hazardous industries and highlights the urgent need for robust safety regulations, effective enforcement, and corporate accountability. Bhopal stands as a powerful testament to the potential human cost when these crucial elements are overlooked or disregarded.

The legacy of Bhopal also serves as a rallying cry for justice and the pursuit of corporate responsibility. The survivors, their families, and countless activists have relentlessly fought for compensation, healthcare, and environmental remediation, challenging powerful interests and pushing for systemic change. Their unwavering determination sends a resounding message that those responsible must be held accountable, and the rights of the victims must be acknowledged and respected.

Furthermore, the Bhopal Gas Tragedy has spurred a broader global conversation about industrial safety, environmental protection, and social justice. It has ignited the passions of activists, academics, and concerned citizens, driving advocacy and influencing policy discussions worldwide. Lessons learned from Bhopal have prompted legislative reforms, improved corporate practices, and a greater emphasis on community well-being and the preservation of the environment.

The enduring legacy of Bhopal also lies in the resilience and strength of the survivors. Their stories of survival, perseverance, and resilience inspire countless others facing adversity. The survivors have transformed their trauma into a catalyst for change, becoming voices of empowerment and advocates for a world free from industrial disasters.

As we reflect on the legacy of Bhopal, it is imperative that we never forget the lives lost and the suffering endured. We must honor their memory by taking proactive steps to prevent similar tragedies in the future. This means holding corporations accountable, demanding robust safety regulations, investing in community resilience, and prioritizing the well-being of people and the environment above profits.

Bhopal will forever serve as a somber reminder of the consequences of negligence, the pursuit of justice, and the power of collective action. It is a story that compels us to learn, to challenge, and to strive for a world where tragedies like Bhopal become relics of the past.

A Call to Action - Improving Industrial Safety and Corporate Responsibility

THE BHOPAL GAS TRAGEDY serves as a powerful catalyst for change, urging us to take action to prevent similar disasters and to hold corporations accountable for their actions. It highlights the critical need for improved industrial safety practices and enhanced corporate responsibility. As we conclude this book, let us delve into some key calls to action that can help foster a safer and more responsible industrial landscape.

1. Strengthening Regulatory Frameworks: Governments worldwide must enact and enforce robust industrial safety regulations that prioritize the protection of human lives and the environment. These regulations should encompass stringent safety standards, regular inspections, and transparent reporting mechanisms. Additionally, governments should allocate adequate resources to regulatory bodies to ensure effective monitoring and enforcement.

2. Enhancing Corporate Responsibility: Corporations have a fundamental duty to prioritize the safety and well-being of their workers, surrounding communities, and the environment. They must invest in comprehensive safety protocols, provide ongoing training to employees, and conduct regular audits to identify and address potential hazards. Furthermore, corporations should embrace transparency, ethical practices, and accountability, taking responsibility for any harm caused by their operations.

3. Promoting Public-Private Partnerships: Governments, civil society organizations, and the private sector should collaborate to promote industrial safety and corporate responsibility. This can involve sharing knowledge, expertise, and resources to develop and implement best practices, facilitate technological advancements, and foster a culture of safety across industries.

4. Supporting Whistleblower Protections: Whistleblowers play a crucial role in uncovering corporate wrongdoing and safety violations. Governments should enact robust legislation to protect whistleblowers, ensuring their anonymity and safeguarding them from retaliation. These protections encourage individuals to come forward with vital information that can prevent potential disasters.

5. Strengthening International Cooperation: Industrial disasters transcend national borders, and global cooperation is essential to address them effectively. Countries should collaborate on sharing best practices, harmonizing safety standards, and establishing international frameworks for corporate accountability. International bodies, such as the United Nations and the International Labour Organization, can play a pivotal role in facilitating dialogue and coordinating efforts.

6. Empowering Communities: Affected communities should be empowered to participate in decision-making processes that impact their lives. Governments and corporations should engage in meaningful dialogue with community representatives, ensuring their voices are heard, and their concerns are taken into account. Community involvement can lead to the development of safer industrial practices and the equitable distribution of resources and benefits.

7. Fostering Public Awareness and Education: Education plays a critical role in promoting a culture of safety and corporate responsibility. Governments, educational institutions, and civil society organizations should integrate industrial safety and corporate ethics into educational curricula, raising awareness from an early age. Public awareness campaigns and media engagement can also contribute to fostering a greater understanding of the importance of safety and accountability.

By taking these calls to action seriously, we can strive towards a future where industrial disasters are minimized, corporate practices prioritize safety and responsibility, and the well-being of communities and the environment is safeguarded.

A Message of Remembrance and Solidarity with the Victims and Survivors

TODAY, WE PAUSE TO remember and honor the victims of the Bhopal Gas Tragedy, a catastrophic event that forever altered the lives of countless individuals and their families. As we reflect on the immense suffering and loss caused by this tragedy, we extend our heartfelt solidarity to the survivors who continue to carry the burden of its aftermath.

OLIVER LANCASTER

To the survivors, we stand with you in your pursuit of justice, accountability, and comprehensive support. Your resilience and unwavering determination in the face of adversity inspire us all. We acknowledge the pain and hardships you have endured, and we join you in demanding that your rights are recognized, your voices heard, and your needs met.

To the families and loved ones who lost their dear ones, we offer our deepest condolences and unwavering support. The void left by the loss of cherished lives can never be filled, but we stand by you in your quest for closure, remembrance, and healing.

The Bhopal Gas Tragedy serves as a somber reminder of the devastating consequences of corporate negligence and the urgency to prioritize human lives and the environment over profit. It calls upon us to work tirelessly towards preventing similar disasters, ensuring robust industrial safety practices, and holding corporations accountable for their actions.

Let us not forget the enduring legacy of Bhopal, for it is a call to action for all of us. Together, we must strive to create a world where every individual is safe in their workplaces, where communities are protected from harm, and where corporate responsibility is upheld as an unwavering commitment.

May our remembrance be a testament to the lives lost and the strength of the survivors. Let us keep their stories alive, carry their voices forward, and work hand in hand to build a future where tragedies like Bhopal become lessons learned, driving us towards a safer, more just, and compassionate world.

THE BHOPAL GAS TRAGEDY: UNRAVELING THE CATASTROPHE OF 1984

In remembrance and solidarity, we stand with the victims, survivors, and their families, united in our commitment to justice, compassion, and a brighter tomorrow.

OLIVER LANCASTER

Sign up to my free newsletter to get updates on new releases, FREE teaser chapters to upcoming releases and FREE digital short stories.

Or visit https://tinyurl.com/olanc

I never spam and you can unsubscribe at any time.

Don't miss out!

Visit the website below and you can sign up to receive emails whenever Oliver Lancaster publishes a new book. There's no charge and no obligation.

https://books2read.com/r/B-A-UNEZ-TUZKC

BOOKS 2 READ

Connecting independent readers to independent writers.

About the Author

Oliver Lancaster possesses an enchanting charm that effortlessly draws readers into the depths of his literary world. With an insatiable curiosity for the unexplained, he skillfully weaves tales of crime, conspiracy, mystery and the unknown, leaving readers on the edge of their seats.

Nestled away in the seclusion of his garden shed, Oliver finds solace and inspiration in the tranquility of nature. Surrounded by greenery and fragrant blooms, he dives into a realm of imagination, unearthing secrets that lie hidden within his mind.

Accompanying Oliver on his literary ventures is his faithful ginger cat named Italics. With his mesmerizing gaze and mysterious mannerisms, Italics adds an air of intrigue to Oliver's writing process, often curling up on a cushioned chair nearby, watching as words flow effortlessly from his human companion's pen.

When not engrossed in his craft, Oliver indulges in the gentle warmth of his garden with a glass of red wine.

Prepare to be spellbound as you delve into the pages of Oliver Lancaster's novels, for he is a master of the eerie, a weaver of secrets, and an unrivaled guide through the labyrinthine corridors of the human psyche.

Sign up to a free newsletter to get updates on new releases, FREE teaser chapters to upcoming releases and FREE digital short stories.

Read more at https://tinyurl.com/olanc.

Printed in the USA
CPSIA information can be obtained
at www.ICGtesting.com
LVHW022303220524
781161LV00032B/813